carefree quilts

a free-style twist on classic designs

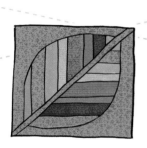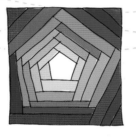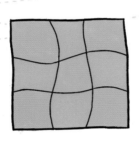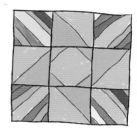

Joy-Lily

KRAUSE PUBLICATIONS
Cincinnati, Ohio

Contents

Welcome to Carefree Quilting!

The credo of this book is *Perfection is Optional*! I believe that quilting should always be enjoyable and relaxing. If you are a novice quilter, the projects in this book are designed to help you feel comfortable while making something you'll love. Consecutive projects will gradually help you improve your piecing and quilt finishing skills. Meanwhile you will become familiar with several traditional quilt block designs.

All twelve block designs in this book have been student-tested. They are somewhat loosey-goosey on purpose—this casual look will provide you freedom from frustration when you sew the blocks. Be sure to follow the cutting instructions carefully; there is a tiny bit of extra fabric in each of the measurements to allow wiggle room in your ¼" seams. After sewing together each block, you will trim it to the exact size, so all the blocks will fit together just right. This is a new, more quilter-friendly type of patchwork instruction. So if you are an experienced quilter, you are in for a treat—more fun and less stress. If you are new to quilting, the forgiving techniques in this book make it a perfect primer for you.

Turn on your sewing machine and become a carefree quilter!

Joy-Lily

4

CHAPTER 1

Start Here:
Tools, Rules, Tips and Tricks

Writing a book that is fresh and interesting to experienced quilters and, at the same time, offers the basics of quilting to newbies is one of my challenges here. It's the same challenge I face several times a week teaching my mixed-level quilt classes. If you are completely new to quilting, be sure to read this chapter before beginning your first project. It will help you with burning issues like what kind of fabric to buy, what kind of thread to use and how to handle your sewing machine when it has a tantrum. This chapter is also full of little hints that will make your first project fun and successful.

If you are a quilter who has been around the cutting table a few times, you may find some useful new information here—or perhaps a good laugh. Take what you like, and do the rest your own way.

Before You Begin . . .

Start Smart

The order of blocks in this book begins with the easiest one (Snow Flower block, page 28) and increases gradually in complexity with each new block in the same chapter. Along the way are two different techniques for sewing patchwork. The first project section of the book shows you the Sew, Flip and Trim method (page 26). The second section teaches you the Stack, Slice, Swap and Sew method (page 60). The third section, Combination Blocks (page 86), blends elements from earlier blocks for three totally new block designs and a full sampler quilt.

Take a break from any perfectionist tendencies you may have while sewing these blocks. If the points get lopped off or the corners don't exactly match, that's part of the playful charm of these projects. As Lisa Boyer says in her hilarious book *That Dorky Homemade Look: Quilting Lessons from a Parallel Universe*, "Oh well, no one will notice." But do check the measurements carefully before you cut fabric.

They are calculated to give you a stress-free experience while making each block and project.

Hand piecing was the only patchwork option until the middle of the nineteenth century when the sewing machine was invented. Those quilters were early adopters of the new machinery—they took to machine sewing as soon as they could! The piecing in this book is intended entirely for machine sewing. The edges get trimmed in the final step of sewing each block, so hand-stitching would come loose. If you love the feel or meditation of hand sewing, you can always finish your quilts with hand quilting. Hand quilting gives your project a soft "maker's hand" look. See pages 112–121 for more information on completing your project.

Quilters' Math

Each of the quilt blocks in this book trims into a 12½" square. Several of the projects like the WALK IN THE PARK TABLE RUNNER (page 28) and the MOONGLOW BABY QUILT (page 34) also include 6½" mini-blocks. In many other projects, instructions for optional mini-blocks are given in sidebars. Because all twelve block designs are the same two sizes, they are all interchangeable. For example, you can use the Wacky Web blocks instead of the Snow Flower blocks to make the table runner (page 28), or use twenty Roman Snake blocks (page 94) to make a bed quilt instead of a pillow. You can use four mini-blocks to replace any full-size block. The number of possible block and project choices is astronomical. Get creative!

If you decide to sew each of the twelve blocks once, you will actually end up with nineteen blocks (this is quilters' math); the process of cutting and sewing blocks with the Stack, Slice, Swap and Sew method usually makes two blocks at once. The Four Play block (page 62) makes four! Sew up one additional block for a total of twenty—that's enough blocks to put together a four by five block sampler quilt like the one on page 108.

Don't worry about figuring out how much fabric you need for each project; I've done that math for you and added a little surplus yardage in case of cutting exuberance.

Quilt for Joy, Not to Order

You'll likely want to make quilts for other people, but be sure to enjoy yourself and have a stress-free experience. If you decide to make a quilt for someone else, I strongly recommend that you discourage specific requests. Be vague about what colors they will get. Please yourself first, because you will be interacting closely with these colors and designs for a while.

Avoid working to deadlines, too. If the baby arrives before the quilt, he or she won't really know the difference. (Call me a cynic, but I don't make wedding quilts until several years after the marriage ceremony.) If a gift quilt for a birthday, Hanukah, Christmas or Father's Day is not done on time, give the recipient a photo of the work in progress. Think how delighted he or she will be when the actual gift arrives at an unexpected moment.

Remember to have fun. Be creative, and quilt for your own pleasure. Get started now for a satisfying and possibly lifelong passion of making beautiful, lovingly-stitched quilts.

Necessary Tools and How to Use Them

You will need all of the tools explained in this section to complete the projects in this book.

Rotary Cutting Tools

- Rotary cutter
- Self-healing cutting mat
- Quilters' ruler

The rotary cutter is the best tool ever invented for quilters! This tool looks like a pizza cutter and has a razor-sharp blade that will slice with precision through several layers of fabric. It cuts quilt pieces better than any scissors. Use it with a clearly marked, heavy plastic quilters' ruler, and cut only on a self-healing cutting mat to produce the strips, squares, triangles and curves called for in this book. An 18" × 24" mat is an appropriate size for most quilting projects. A 24" × 6½" ruler is the most versatile size.

Rotary cutters are constantly being improved. Some are self-closing, and some have trigger handles or easy blade-changing features. One style is ergonomically shaped for people with arthritis. (See the Resources section on page 124.) Most rotary cutters can be used by a left-hander (like me) by switching the blade to the other side. Rotary cutters, rulers and mats are often packaged together in three-piece kits for easy shopping.

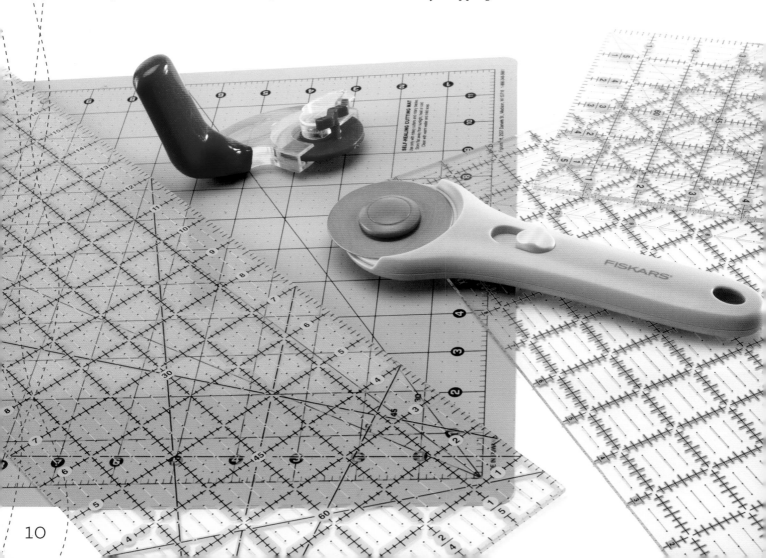

Using Your Rotary Cutting Tools

CLEAN UP THE EDGE

Always cut strips and pieces from a cleanly trimmed edge of fabric. To clean up an irregular edge, fold the yardage in half with the selvages lined up. Put the selvages on a horizontal line at the top or bottom of the cutting board. Place a 90-degree cross line on the ruler along the selvages. Keep it aligned while moving the ruler as far toward the edge as needed to cut off the irregular bit (Figure 1).

CUT THE STRIPS

First rotate the freshly cleaned-up fabric 180 degrees around the board (or just rotate the board). To cut a 2" strip, for example, put the strip ruler over the cut edge of the fabric. Line up the cut fabric edge along the 2" vertical line on the ruler. When you cut at the zero edge of the ruler, the piece underneath will be the 2" strip you want. It is protected from accidental slicing during the cutting. For strips and pieces larger than the ruler's width, use the lines on the cutting board. Whenever possible, cut with the ruler protecting the piece you want to use.

CUTTING IS A TWO-HANDED ACTION

To cut, place the blade snuggly against the ruler edge at the bottom of the fabric. Always cut upward, away from your body. (As necessary, rotate the board before cutting a different side so the cut will always be going upward and away from you.) Begin cutting with your ruler-holding hand about 8" above the bottom of the fabric edge with your five fingertips poised on the ruler, away from the blade. Be sure to use plenty of strength in both hands: one to make the cut and the other to keep the ruler in position (Figure 2). Pause when the blade is next to the fingertips of your ruler hand. Leave the blade in place. Without moving the ruler, carefully move your ruler hand up another few inches, and then continue the cut (Figure 3). This way you will be in complete control of the blade.

BE SHARP, BE SAFE!

Practice cutting with one or two layers of fabric. Change blades often, especially if the blade skips part of the cut. Make a habit of closing the blade every time you put the cutter down.

Figure 1: Clean up the raw edge first.

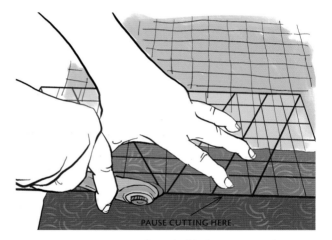

PAUSE CUTTING HERE.

Figure 2: Pause cutting when the blade is next to the fingertips of your ruler hand.

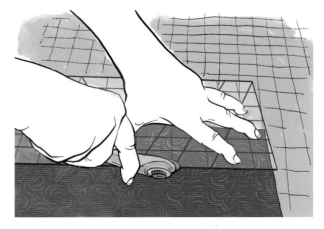

Figure 3: Move hand up, then continue to cut.

Sewing Machine

The kind of sewing machine to buy is a very personal choice. If you already have a machine, keeping it running or repairing it is usually a better strategy than buying a new one.

Parts inside newer machines are mostly plastic; if a part breaks and the manufacturer no longer supplies it, you have instant landfill. Older machines with metal parts can always be fixed, even if a new part needs to be fabricated. If you are buying a new machine, look for a few important features: variable needle positions, a good light, portability and standard accessories. Once you know whether your machine has a low or high needle shank for attaching the feet, you can buy standard versions of various feet. However, with the more expensive machine brands, you must use the same brand of feet, bobbins and accessories. Adjustable presser foot tension is desirable (see Undercover Stripping on page 23) but seldom available.

One feature available on electronic machines that I wish I had on my twenty-five year old electric machine (used to sew the projects in this book) is the "stop needle down" setting. This setting automatically puts your needle in the down position (or up position, if you prefer) whenever you stop sewing. Try out as many machines as you can before buying one to determine which features you need and which features are unnecessary.

Thread

Medium-gray thread is a convenient color for most patchwork, but what *kind* of thread you use in your sewing machine is important; it can effect the way your machine performs. If your machine is an American or Asian brand, it is engineered to use American brands of thread. European machines are designed to use European threads (see Resources page 124). These different threads are spun in opposite directions. (On 4-ply knitting yarn, you can actually see the twist, but it is there on sewing thread, too.) Thread with the wrong twist direction leaves tiny particles (shaved-off bumps from the backward twist) in your machine, eventually gumming it up. The thread also gets weaker when the bumps are shaved off. Bargain bin thread is no good at all for use in sewing machines or for quilted keepsakes, but it's acceptable for basting.

Five Easy Fixes for a Cranky Sewing Machine

If your sewing machine isn't working properly, try these five suggestions before you lug it to a mechanic:

- Use the correct type of thread for your brand of machine. The bobbin thread should be the same type as the top thread.

- Strong, tight stitches have equal amounts of tension pulling from the top thread and from the bobbin. To check the stitch tension, sew two layers of fabric together and then pull the layers open. If the tension is loose, the stitches will gap and wiggle. (Loose stitches are called *hen's teeth* in quilt jargon.) To correct this, put contrasting colors of thread in the top and bobbin. If your stitched sample has tiny dots of the top color on its under side, the top tension is too weak against the pull of the bobbin; gradually dial up the number on the thread tension knob, located somewhere above the needle, until the dots nearly vanish. If the bottom thread is leaving dots on top, dial it down. If your machine has a bobbin case, the bobbin tension can be adjusted by slightly turning the tiny set screw on the side of the case.

- Change the needle. To find out if your needle is dull, gently run your finger under the tip. If you feel any roughness, change it. If it looks even slightly bent, change it. If the machine begins to skip stitches or the thread breaks, an old needle is often the cause. For sewing on quilt fabrics, use size 80/12 or 90/14 needles. For machine quilting a project, always begin with a fresh needle.

- Check that the bobbin thread is in its tension slot and is unspooling in the correct direction. If you are in doubt about the correct direction, try both. One way will make better stitches. (Your sewing machine owner's manual or a diagram on the machine may also reveal the correct direction.)

- To stop the machine from balking at the beginning of a seam, grab the leading threads. Pull them firmly behind the machine as you begin to sew. The presser foot works well only when it is level, so if you have a very thick seam, trick the foot by folding a small pad of fabric as thick as the seam. Put this pad under the back of the presser foot before you begin sewing the seam to keep the foot level.

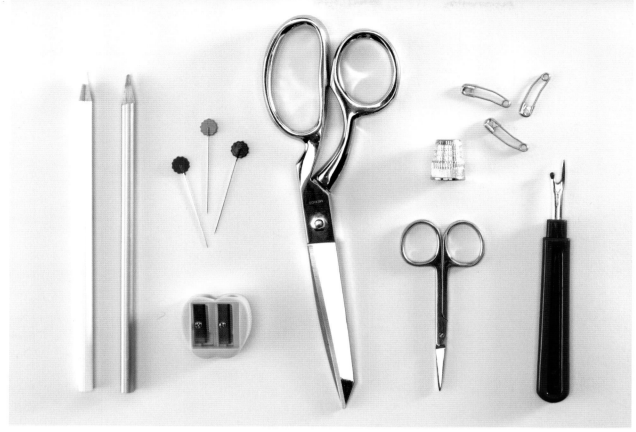

Shown above are a few of the basic tools every quilter should have in the workroom.

Seam Ripper

A simple seam ripper with a small handle and hook-shaped cutting end is the most important tool in your kit. Yes, you will need to rip sometimes, but it will be carefree with the clever ripping technique on page 22.

Painters Blue Masking Tape

This particular type of tape leaves no residue on your fabric so it is perfect for marking quilting lines and for holding down the backing fabric when you make a quilt sandwich. (See page 116 for quilt assembly.)

Scissors and Snippers

It's helpful to have two pairs of scissors on hand: fabric scissors and paper scissors. Fabric scissors are extremely sharp and cut through fabric beautifully; to keep them sharp, only use them to cut fabric. Paper scissors need not be as sharp as your fabric scissors. Use them for cutting paper templates.

It's handy to have a pair of thread snippers or tiny scissors at your sewing machine. Use them to clip thread tails close to the fabric as it comes through the machine.

Drawing Supplies

It's very helpful to have some drawing supplies on hand and available while working on a project. Several of the projects in this book require that you draw a template shape on the fabric prior to cutting. You'll need regular or mechanical pencils with soft lead, as well as a white or silver pencil for drawing visible lines on dark fabric. Keep a pencil sharpener handy—a sharp pencil will produce more accurate lines than a dull one. Finally, a white vinyl eraser will remove stray pencil lines easily without leaving smudges on the fabric.

Templates can be made of file folder cardboard or from thin, rigid template plastic available from quilting notions suppliers (see Resources page 124).

Other Standard Tools

Every quilter will need quilt pins, curved basting safety pins, a steam iron for pressing seams and an ironing pad or board. I also recommend having a thimble that fits your middle finger; it is extremely helpful when doing any hand-stitching.

Optional Tools and Materials

You may already have some of these tools, or you can put them on your birthday-gift wish list. Many are easily found in the notions section of craft and sewing stores, or in catalogs. They make quilting even easier, but none are critical to the projects in this book.

Magnetic Pin Holder

Pins find these holders irresistible. You'll find pins easily when you need them.

Water-Soluble Marker

Mark stitching patterns on your quilt top with this pen. After stitching, remove the lines with a damp cloth.

Digital Camera

Look at groups of fabrics with the grayscale feature on your camera to reveal the different values among them. To see the whole quilt layout at once, look at it through the camera. It works like a reducing glass. Keep a photo record of block layouts and finished quilts. (For more uses of a digital camera in quilting, see page 24.)

Daylight Lamp

Direct sunlight is the best light for working. You can have sunlight at night too with a color-corrected daylight lamp.

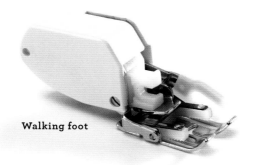

Walking foot

Flannel-Backed Plastic Tablecloth

Organize the blocks for a quilt on the flannel side of a plastic tablecloth, and then roll it up to carry or store your work. (See page 24 for information on making a flannel board which serves a similar purpose for individual blocks.)

Small Craft Knife/Smallest Rotary Cutter

Either of these cutting tools is better than scissors for making accurate cardboard or plastic templates. Always cut on a self-healing cutting board.

Fusible Products and Pressing Sheet

Thin interfacing with one-sided, iron-on glue is useful for several projects in this book. The ZIGZAG TOTE BAG (page 52) is made with heavier, craft-weight fusible interfacing which provides additional body.

One project uses fusible web—an all glue, gossamer material that goes by names like Wonder-Under, Stitch Witchery and Misty Fuse (see Resources page 124). Fusible web is great for appliqué and for sealing two fabrics together. Always protect your iron and work surface from the melting glue with parchment paper (available in supermarkets near the aluminum foil) or a Teflon pressing sheet.

Walking Foot

When you quilt a project on your sewing machine (page 119), a walking foot (sometimes called an *even-feed foot*) keeps the three layers of fabric and batting running smoothly together through the machine. (Use it for straight-line quilting only, not free-motion quilting.)

Flexible Tape Measure

Measuring a contoured surface such as a pillow or a person is easier with a flexible tape than with a ruler. I suggest purchasing one that is at least 60" long.

Transparent Red and Green Plastic Cards

Take these cards to the fabric store to discern different values of fabrics (see Resources page 124).

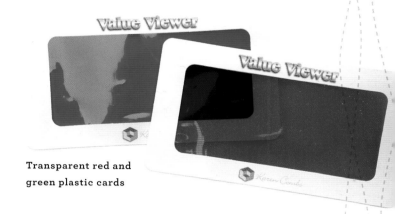

Transparent red and green plastic cards

Table Extension

Make the working surface of your machine much bigger and make your piecing and quilting easier with one of these accessories. It will need to fit snugly around your machine.

Bicycle Cuff Clamps

Cyclists use these C-shaped metal clamps to hold their pants away from the bike. Quilters use them to keep the quilt rolled up during quilting (see drawing on page 119).

Hand Calculator

It's easy to figure out yardages needed when you don't have to do long division. (See page 120 for a simple formula that helps you calculate how much binding fabric to buy.)

12½" Square Quilters' Ruler

This is the perfect tool for trimming the finished blocks exactly to size. Use the inner lines to cut the 6½" blocks too.

18" Revolving Cutting Mat

Trimming the 12½" blocks is especially easy when you rotate this mat to cut each side.

Spray Starch

If you prewash your fabric (see page 18 for more information), use a little spray starch when ironing it. Starch brings back the original crispness of the fabric, making the fabric easier to cut and sew.

There are many other toys, and more are invented all the time. When you peruse quilting supply catalogs or visit major quilt shows, you can't miss them!

Spray starch

Quilting Rules

As in life, in quilting a few rules are absolutely necessary to avoid chaos and make a quilt come together. Other rules can simplify the process or make you feel more comfortable. Beware of assuming rules like "Seams must always be pressed open." Not all rules are really necessary. And don't get bogged down with too many rules. This section is divided into two parts: my rules (the rules you should follow when using this book) and your rules (the rules you make for yourself).

My Rules

Sewing by the Numbers

Quarter inch seams are the standard for seam allowances in quilting. Fabric yardage and cutting measurements are usually specified assuming that all seams are sewn exactly $\frac{1}{4}$" from the cut edge of the fabric. (Once upon a time, it was $\frac{1}{4}$" minus the thickness of the thread!) This book is no exception to the $\frac{1}{4}$" seam rule, but I have found that depending on the weather, my mood and other ineffable factors, *my* $\frac{1}{4}$" is not the same every time! To keep the instructions carefree, I have added a tiny bit extra into the fabric requirements and cutting numbers for each block in this book. The last instruction for each block is "trim to $12\frac{1}{2}$" (or $6\frac{1}{2}$" for the mini-blocks). So whether your $\frac{1}{4}$" seams are always just right or are a moving target like mine, your finished blocks will all wind up the same size. Whew!

Because of this, you do have to pay close attention to the cutting numbers and to position your ruler carefully when cutting. (This is lots easier than sewing perfect $\frac{1}{4}$" seams.) The amount of fabric listed for each project is a bit more than you actually need because "slice happens."

There are several ways to get a consistent $\frac{1}{4}$" seam. Some machines have a setting for it or a universally adjustable needle that you can line up exactly $\frac{1}{4}$" from the edge of the presser foot. Several styles of presser feet are available with special raised or marked $\frac{1}{4}$" edges. A strip of thick tape (like rug tape) on the machine table $\frac{1}{4}$" from the needle provides a guide for the fabric. A repositionable magnetic seam guide is useful on older machines with metal sewing surfaces. With a tricky piece to sew, the best bet may be to draw a $\frac{1}{4}$" line directly on the fabric to follow. Whichever way you find best to produce $\frac{1}{4}$" seams, watch the edge of the fabric as you sew, not the needle.

Choosing Quilt Fabrics

Use quilt fabric only. My first quilt was made of rayon satin. It was a mess and so was I! The correct fabric for making quilts is 100-percent cotton broadcloth with a fairly tight weave (around 75–80 threads per inch), but not as tight as bedsheet fabric (which starts around 200 threads per inch). Quilt fabric is much easier to cut and sew than other fabrics, so I use it exclusively for all my pieced quilting.

Quilting fabric is typically 42"–44" wide. You'll see it for sale folded in half to 21"–22" wide and wrapped around a bolt. Fat quarters, specified a few times in this book, are 22" × 18" cuts of fabric—a more useful quarter yard shape than 9" × 42". However, if you need more fabric, buying it cut from the bolt will cost less per yard than buying several fat quarters. Yardage requirements in this book are based on 40"-wide fabric to allow for possible shrinkage (see page 18 for more information on prewashing).

Thousands of designs and colors are available in fabric made especially for quilters. Some fabrics have quite large print patterns. Use the big print patterns only for very large blocks or wide borders, as in the GARDEN PATH QUILT (page 74). In general, small print fabrics that look solid at a distance work best for the projects in this book. When you are close up, the texture is a nice additional element. (The cover shows some tiny print fabrics close up.) Most of the quilts in this book are actually made with textured or patterned fabric, even if they look like solid colors at first glance.

If you have some special fabric you want to use in a quilt but it doesn't conform to these rules about type of fabric and pattern size, go ahead and use it, but try making the project in cotton first.

Press a seam open.

Press a seam to the side.

Pressing Seams and Just Plain Pressing

Open or closed seams—this is a huge debate among quilters. Pressing all seams open is a lot more work. Sometimes it's a good idea, such as when joining long, skinny strips or bulky seams. But unless the instructions say specifically to press them open, always press seams to one side, preferably toward the darker fabric. Sometimes a seam will be twisted after it's been sewn in at both ends. Don't fret—this twist will be inside the quilt where nobody will see it. Just press the seam open near the middle.

After pressing the seams on the back, check the front for any inadvertent folds and press them out. An iron with the jet steam feature is far superior for quilting than a regular steam iron. All of these instructions say *press*, not *iron*. The difference is that ironing means gliding the iron back and forth over a wide swath. Pressing means placing the iron directly on the part you want to flatten—up and down—and maybe giving it a jet of steam.

Choosing Batting

Quilts are actually quite thin bed covers. The fat, fluffy ones are called comforters, and they are typically tied together (see page 117). Fat batting is not recommended for quilt stitching; it's too bulky. Originally, quilts were filled with hand-carded wool or cotton. They needed a lot of stitches to keep the stuffing from sliding around and lumping up during washing. Nowadays, battings are engineered to avoid shifting and lumping, so you can safely space the stitching lines a hand's width apart or more.

Batting is available in cotton, bamboo, silk, polyester, blends and even wool. Some kinds come in packages only, others are sold by the yard. Thin batting is about the thickness of craft felt but softer. (Go ahead and use that leftover felt in place of batting.) I especially like the Warm & Natural and Warm & White brands of batting by the yard because leftover scraps can be zigzag-stitched together, butting the edges. When the join is steam-pressed, it becomes perfectly flat. (Don't press polyester batting—it melts.)

There are also fusible battings that replace basting with pressing. Try fusible batting in a small project before using it in a full-sized quilt.

Your Rules

Quilters love to make rules. They give order to our quilts and our work habits. They usually serve a sensible purpose. Some rules are very personal or quirky. For example, my mother never sewed on dark colors at night. I know quilters who always press after sewing each seam (I don't). Traditional Log Cabin blocks always start with a red square in the middle to symbolize the hearth of the home. One of my rules is to bind a quilt with the same fabric I used for the outer border. It's a useful aesthetic rule, but I've broken it several times in this book because I thought something else looked better. Also, I ran out of matching fabric once! The point is that rules (mine or yours) are intended to help you. When they constrain or annoy you, or using them doesn't please you, break them!

To Wash or Not to Wash the Fabric

The most frequent question I get from new quilters is "Should I prewash my fabrics before making them into a quilt?" The answer is: It depends. Cotton shrinks a bit when washed in hot water, so if you are making something you expect will be washed a lot, like a baby quilt or place mats, definitely prewash the yardage before you cut it. For a small wall quilt that will probably never be washed, you can skip prewashing. If you have a sensitivity to chemicals in the sizing of new fabrics, of course you'll want to wash them out.

I don't wash my fabrics because, frankly, I'm lazy. My excuses are:

- I can't wait to get started.

- Most of my quilts are for display rather than hard use. When I give someone a bed quilt, I admonish them to wash it infrequently and only in cold water.

- I really like the crisp feel of new fabrics.

- I don't like ironing yardage. If you wash all of your fabric, you'll need to iron it (maybe with a little spray starch) before using it.

Decide for yourself whether to prewash or not. Everyone has different priorities.

One or Several Projects?

"Finish one before you start another" is a rule for some quilters. Not me! I always have several projects in progress. I design my quilts as I go along, so sometimes I'm stumped on what's next with a particular project. While I wait for my muse to tell me the answer, I keep quilting—on something else. I call this "productive procrastination."

You'll know which way this rule works best for you. Don't feel guilty when you choose to break it.

Storing Works in Progress

If you tend to have several projects half done (quilters call those PHD's) at the same time, you will need a storage system to keep the bits and pieces of each project organized. Clean, unused pizza boxes are perfect for finding a PHD easily when the muse speaks. A medium-size pizza box is big enough to hold a stack of completed blocks, templates, matching thread and more. Stack the boxes flat, and label the front edges for easy identification.

For larger projects, lay out the blocks on the flannel side of a flannel-backed plastic tablecloth, roll it up and store it away (page 24).

A lateral file cabinet—the kind that shows all the files sideways when the drawer is open—is another great organizing system for quilting. Use an expanding pocket file folder for each project. When you open the drawer, all projects are instantly at your fingertips. And they all disappear when you close it.

Stashing Fabric

Owning beautiful fabric is one of the great treats of being a quilter. A stash of quilt fabric is both art material and collectible at the same time. It's also a great ongoing rationale for shopping—you can never have too much quilt fabric! Sometimes I buy fabric for a particular project, and sometimes I "need" a fabric just because it's beautiful. When the fabric literally begins to pile up, you'll need to decide how to organize and display your stash. Some people sort by color and arrange their stash in a rainbow array. Some organize their stash by fabric type: reproductions, batiks, calicos, solids, etc. Organize your fabrics by categories that make them easy for you to find. Keep all fabrics out of direct sunlight to avoid fading.

Think Out of the Box

Who says quilts have to be rectangles? Throw away that rule and create interesting new quilts like this one, called HAPPY COAT. Made of three blocks in the book, HAPPY COAT is arranged in an original way.

Fabric Colors

The second most asked question is "How do I choose colors for my quilt?" Whole books are written on this subject alone. I recommend browsing through *The Magical Effects of Color* by Joen Wolfrom for more ideas and strategies on choosing colors. Color preference is very personal. Some people prefer bold, bright colors; others prefer soothing, quiet colors. Sometimes you want a quilt to reflect a mood or a decorating scheme. A quilt could also be the inspiration for planning your decor. A few basic concepts about color can help organize your thinking about color choices for a great looking quilt.

Contrast and Proportion

- **Contrast** is the difference between lighter and darker values of color. Between black and white, the human eye can discern about ten different shades of gray. Books on color theory use a scale of ten to twelve grays. Every color has a value somewhere on this gray scale. To see the values of the fabrics you select for your quilt, set your digital camera to show only black and white. To create contrast in your quilt, use values at least two steps apart on the gray scale. They may range all the way from darkest to lightest values or only encompass a part of the range. You may use several fabrics of the same value in one quilt—just not right next to each other. If you don't have a digital camera, place a pair of transparent red and green plastic cards or cellophane over a group of fabrics to reveal their relative values.

- **Proportion** is how much of each color or value you use. One color or value should be dominant, with another one or two colors or values used in lesser amounts.

    In the WILD GOOSE CHASE WALL QUILT on the cover and page 46, very light values predominate. There are a fair amount of very dark values of magenta, browns and greens. Medium green is the accent and binding color.

    Tiny amounts of a surprising accent color such as the yellow in the SQUARE DANCE QUILT (page 62) can add sparkle or drama to your quilt.

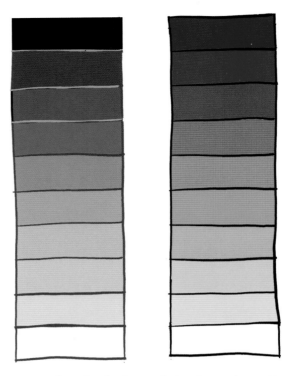

Gray scale and red value gradation (monochromatic color scheme)

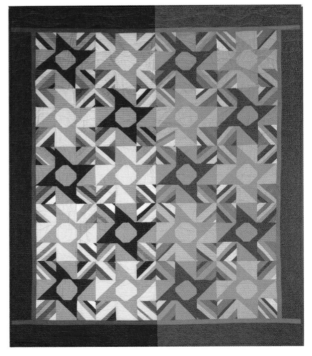

HEAT WAVE QUILT (page 88) in color and gray scale

Color Schemes

Following a color scheme based on the color wheel can simplify choosing colors. Here is a one-page lesson on color schemes.

- **Monochromatic** means only one color. All values light to dark and all tones bright to neutral of a single color make a soothing looking quilt. Blue-and-white quilts are in this tradition, but rose reds, pinks and wines look good together, too. Try variations of any single color.

- **Triads** are any three colors equidistant on the twelve-color wheel. The primary colors (red, yellow and blue) are the most familiar triad, but others like green, orange and violet in varied values look great together, too.

- **Complementary colors** are directly across from each other on the color wheel, like red and green. Used full strength (called pure hues), red and green may be suitable for a Christmas quilt. Using lighter values of red (pinks) and toned-down darker greens will look more like a garden, but they are still red and green!

- **Analogous colors** are next-door neighbors on the color wheel. The CAREFREE SAMPLER QUILT (page 108) is made of analogous colors—blues, blue-violets, purples, red-violets and pinks in various values.

- **Analogous-complementary color schemes** include the complement of one of the analogous colors. WILD GOOSE CHASE WALL QUILT (page 46) has analogous colors—violet, red-violet, brown, dark red, red-orange and also green, the complement of red.

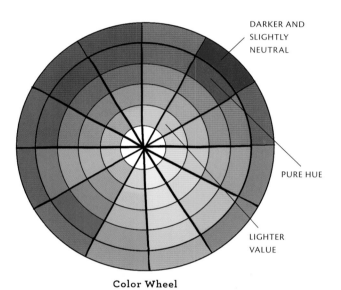

DARKER AND SLIGHTLY NEUTRAL

PURE HUE

LIGHTER VALUE

Color Wheel

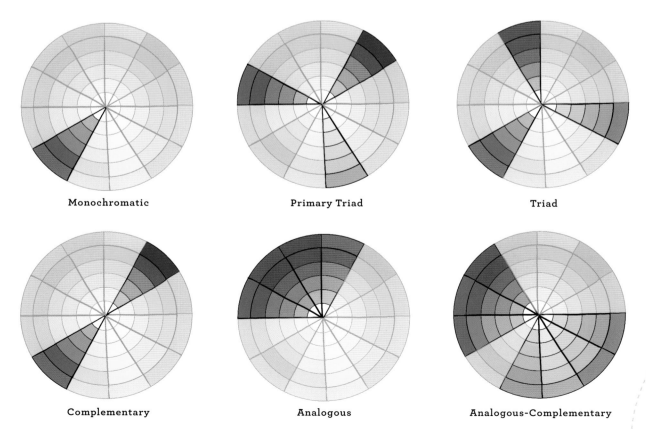

Monochromatic

Primary Triad

Triad

Complementary

Analogous

Analogous-Complementary

Tips and Tricks

Some of these tips reappear in specific quilt instructions as needed. Others apply generally to your quilting. Some are for very specific situations.

Be a Happy Ripper

To rip seams without stress to either the fabric or the quilter, use a hook-ended seam ripper. With the fabric laying flat, slide the pointed end of the ripper under a stitch and push it forward until the blade in the curve cuts a stitch. Repeat this every three to four stitches across the whole line of stitching you need to rip. Turn the fabric over and catch a stitch with the ripper. When you pull the back thread—voilà!—the whole row of stitches will release. For the projects in this book, set your machine for ten to twelve stitches per inch, and you'll rip as easily as you sew.

Rip every three to four stitches.

Matching Seams Like Fun

On many of the projects in this book, the place where a pair of blocks comes together is the same color. If the seams don't match exactly, it will only be visible on the finished work with a microscope! Matching only one seam, as in the COCKTAIL APRON (page 40), is easy. A few projects have multiple seams to align, so here are a few tips to make matching them easy too.

- In a row of seams, start by aligning the center seams and match outward.

- The stitching will actually join $\frac{1}{4}$" below the raw edge, so check the alignment $\frac{1}{4}$" deep, not at the edge.

- With seam allowances pressed to one side, lay one pair to the left and the other to the right. When two seams don't quite match up, try flipping both pairs of seam allowances to the opposite sides. Because the fabric thickness is a factor, this will either move the seams a bit closer or farther apart.

- Pin the matched seams extensively so they won't shift during sewing.

- If nothing else helps, sew a long, thin wedge in the slack seam.

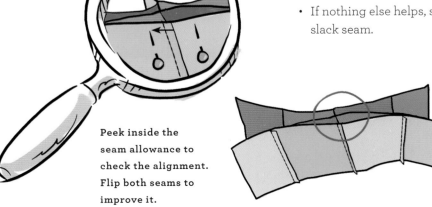

Peek inside the seam allowance to check the alignment. Flip both seams to improve it.

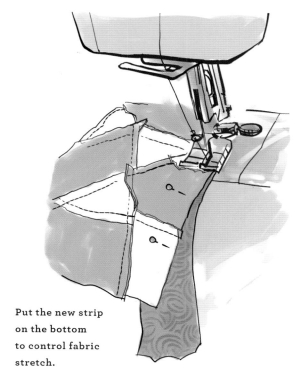

Put the new strip on the bottom to control fabric stretch.

Undercover Stripping

You will frequently need to sew strips onto the edge of a larger piece. The obvious way do this would be to sew with the new strip on top of the larger piece, but that's not the best plan. Although the presser foot holds the top fabric down firmly, it also causes the fabric to drag and stretch just a little. Try one or more of these strategies to help avoid wavy strips and borders:

- When sewing, put the strip on the bottom, not on the top. The little treads under your machine needle are called *feed dogs*; they carry the bottom fabric smoothly forward. This method also means that the seam allowances in the block or quilt will be on top, so you can easily stitch over them in the direction they were pressed.

- Lessen the pressure on the presser foot (if possible on your machine) so the fabric just barely moves forward. Older machines allow you to adjust the presser foot tension with a button at the top. Newer machines seldom have this option, but some machines adjust the tension automatically by computer.

- Use a walking foot (page 14), which is designed to move the top and bottom layers of fabric at the same rate. Keep in mind that this foot is extra wide and may make it harder to maintain a ¼" seam.

- Pin the seam about every inch, perpendicular to the cut edges. Remove each pin just before the needle gets to it—do not ever sew over pins.

- Whenever possible, cut fabric strips parallel to the selvage. The fabric will hardly stretch at all when cut in this direction. (Fabric strips cut perpendicular to the selvage have quite a bit of stretch. Pull a piece of quilt fabric in each direction to see the difference.)

Tricky Biases

Bias is the 45-degree angle between the length and the width of the fabric. Bias-cut fabric can really stretch, so you need to handle and sew it carefully. But fear not! Follow these suggestions to sew bias edges problem-free:

- Sew with the bias-cut fabric piece on the bottom whenever possible. The feed dogs will keep it moving without stretching.

- Avoid using a bias-cut fabric piece at the outside edge of the quilt. (The cutting diagram for the GARDEN PATH QUILT on page 78 looks wasteful, but it is set up to keep a straight grain on the outer edges of the triangles.)

- To keep a long, bias-cut edge in line, fuse a thin strip of lightweight fusible interfacing on the back of it (before cutting, if possible) right where the sewing line will go.

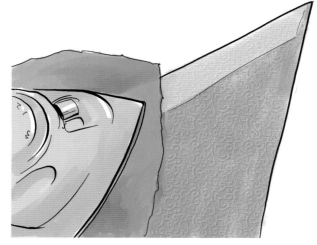

Fuse a thin strip of lightweight fusible interfacing on the back of a bias edge to prevent stretching.

Banish the See-Through Shadows

When a dark color is underneath a very light-colored fabric, the dark fabric may show through. To avoid this, fuse a thin white fabric to the back of the light fabric to make it opaque. See pages 14 and 50 for more information.

Digital Camera Ideas

Your digital camera has many great quilting uses.

- Discern differences in color values by using the black and white setting on your camera to look at various fabrics together.

- View the whole quilt at once through the lens. It will act as a reducing glass and help you get a perspective of the entire project.

- Take photos of the trial layouts of your quilt blocks as a record of what you've tried. Then you can re-create your favorite layout after trying a few other arrangements (or after the cat comes through).

- Keep a memory album or portfolio of the quilts you make and give away.

- Photograph ideas for quilts—color combinations, geometric forms and motifs—anything that inspires you.

View the whole quilt at once through the lens.

Flannel Board and Tablecloth Tricks

- Make a flannel board by wrapping flannel, fuzzier side out, around a piece of plywood or foamcore board. Secure the flannel to the back of the board with tacks, tape or staples. Use this board near your sewing machine to keep quilt pieces in the correct position as you sequentially pick them up and sew them. The fabric will naturally cling to the flannel.

- Use the flannel-back side of a plastic tablecloth to arrange a whole quilt. Put it on a bed with the flannel side up, and lay out the quilt blocks on it. When you need to store the work in progress, carry it to class or take a nap, just roll up the tablecloth. The pieces will unroll exactly where you left them. (I have several PHDs [Projects Half Done] safely stored this way, awaiting the quilting muse.)

More Tips for Carefree Quilting

- Keep a small bottle of hydrogen peroxide handy for removing bloodstains after a pin or needle attacks you.

- When you pause while quilting, cover up your layout of loose quilt pieces before the cat rearranges them.

- As you remove work from the machine, snip the threads close to the end of the seam. You will have many fewer threads to clip later. At the same time, leave long lead threads on the machine so the needle doesn't unthread when you resume sewing. (Some new machines have a thread cutter positioned to leave long lead threads.)

CHAPTER 2

Sew, Flip and Trim Blocks

The blocks in this section are all made using fabric base pieces cut to specific sizes. Simply sew fabrics onto the base fabric, flip them forward into position and press. Then trim any overhanging fabric along the edge of the base fabric piece. It sounds easy because it really is! As long as you take care cutting the base pieces to the correct sizes, each of these blocks will go together like a dream.

If you've never sewn a patchwork block before, the Snow Flower block (the first one in this section) is a great place to start as it is the easiest block in the book. You'll acquire new skills and techniques with each block and project—the complexity of the designs gradually increases but there's no rocket science here!

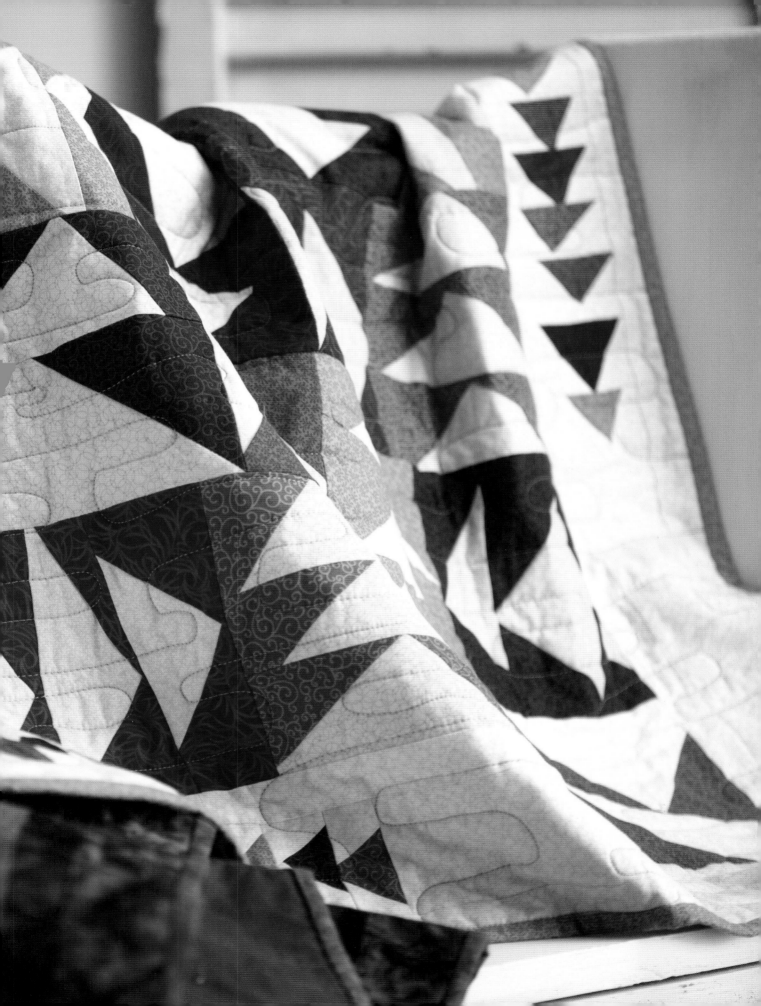

SNOW FLOWER BLOCK

Walk in the Park Table Runner

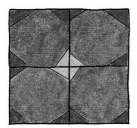

The Snow Flower block is a variation on the traditional Snowball block. By tweaking the corners of the four Snowballs slightly, the flower becomes more natural looking. These blocks go together so fast that you may want to stitch up a whole bunch of them. The table runner is assembled by the pillowcase method (see page 115) which needs no binding. It's a stroll in the park to make.

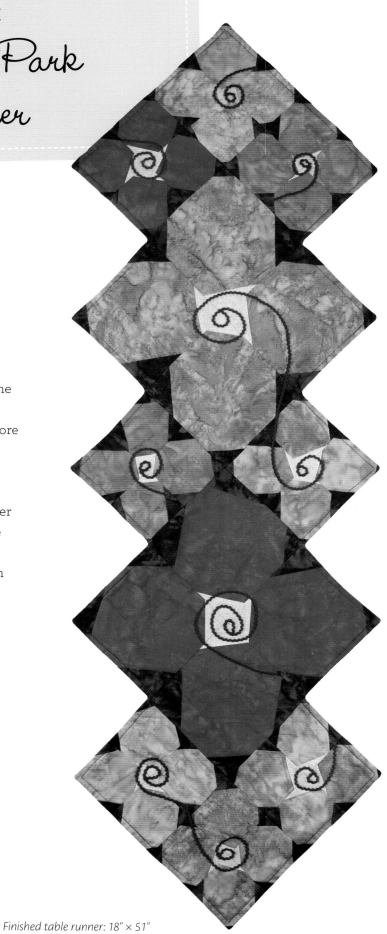

Finished table runner: 18" × 51"

Materials, Tools and Cutting Instructions

FOR A SINGLE BLOCK:

* **¼ yard of bright fabric** (flower petals)
  * Cut four 6¾" squares.

* **Scrap of contrast fabric** (flower center)
  * Cut one 2" × 18" strip.

* **¼ yard of fabric** (background)
  * Cut two 2½" × 42"/44" strips.

TOOLS:

* Basic cutting and sewing tools

FOR THE TABLE RUNNER:

* **¼ yard each of two large flower colors** (makes a large and small flower from each color)
  * From each fabric, cut four 6¾" squares and four 3¾" squares.

* **¼ yard each of three small flower colors** (makes two small flowers from each color)
  * From all three fabrics, cut eight 3¾" squares.

* **¼ yard of yellow fabric** (flower centers)
  * Cut one 2" × 42"/44" strip (large flowers).
  * Cut two 1½" × 42"/44" strips (small flowers).

* **1½ yards of green background fabric**
  * Cut three 2½" × 42"/44" strips (large flowers).
  * Cut two 1½" × 42"/44" strips (small flowers).
  * Reserve the leftover fabric for the back of the runner.

* 20" × 54" of thin batting

* Thread to match background color

* 4 yards of green mini-rickrack

TOOLS:

* Basic cutting and sewing tools

* Fabric turning tool or pointed chopstick

* Hand sewing needle

Make the Snow Flower Block

1 Place a yellow strip on the corner of a flower square, right sides together, leaving a triangle of bottom fabric showing (Figure 1). Position the strip so the top leg of the triangle is a little shorter than the right leg (Figure 2). Sew along the side of the strip that is closest to the corner with a ¼" seam. Repeat for three more flower squares.

Note: Before you sew, make sure that when the sewn strip is flipped over, it will completely cover the triangle.

2 Flip the yellow strips right-side up (Figure 3). Press. Turn each square to the back and trim the yellow strip flush with the edges of the flower square (Figure 4).

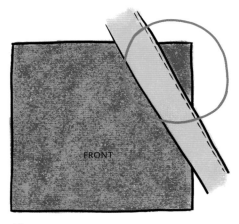

FRONT

Figure 1

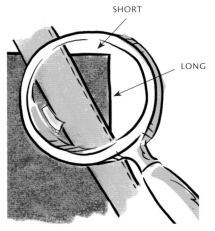

SHORT

LONG

Figure 2

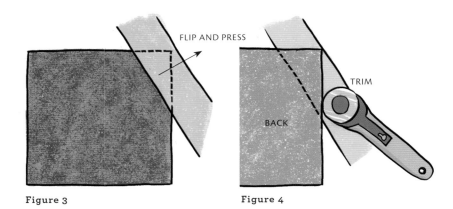

FLIP AND PRESS

BACK

TRIM

Figure 3

Figure 4

Be More Organic

Instead of cutting four 6¾" squares to make one flower, first cut a 13½" square and then divide it into unequal rectangles. This will create a flower seen at an angle. Or make the cuts slightly curved for an even more realistic flower. Sew the curved pieces together with instructions for the Curvy Nine Patch block on page 74. Sewing these curves is easier than it looks. Label the pieces by position (top left, bottom right, etc.) to keep them in the correct spot.

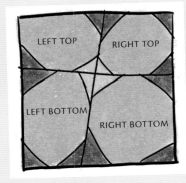

LEFT TOP | RIGHT TOP

LEFT BOTTOM

RIGHT BOTTOM

Unequal rectangles

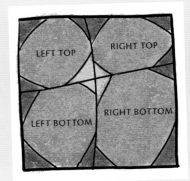

LEFT TOP | RIGHT TOP

LEFT BOTTOM

RIGHT BOTTOM

Curved rectangles

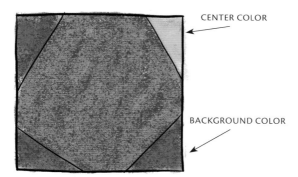

CENTER COLOR

BACKGROUND COLOR

Figure 5

3 With the 2½" strip of background color fabric, repeat steps 1 and 2 on the remaining three corners of all four flower squares (Figure 5). Vary the triangles to achieve a natural flower look. Each triangle should cover about ⅓ of a side. Save any scraps for other corners.

4 Lay out the four trimmed squares with the yellow corners in the center. Sew each pair of squares together with ¼" seams. Join the two units (Figure 6). Matching seams in the middle isn't necessary. Press. Trim the finished block to 12½" square.

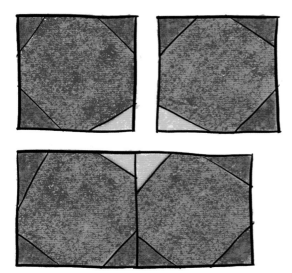

Figure 6

Chain Stitching

Try chain stitching the corners on the flower blocks. Sew only one corner of each square, lined up on a single strip. This is much faster than sewing and cutting each corner individually.

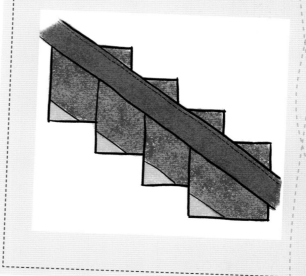

Make the Walk in the Park Table Runner

1 Follow steps 1–4 of the block instructions to make two large flowers and eight small flowers (Figure 1).

2 Trim the large blocks to 12½" square. Trim the mini-blocks to 6½" square.

3 To make the table runner backing, sew together two pieces of background fabric to make a rectangle approximately 20" × 53", just slightly larger than the flower unit (Figure 2). Press the seam open.

4 On top of the batting, place the backing piece right-side up. Center the flower unit right-side down on top of the backing. Pin the three layers together all around.

5 With a ¼" seam, stitch around the inside edge of the flowers unit. Leave a straight 6½" section open for turning the runner out (Figure 3). Keep the needle down in the fabric when turning each of the corners.

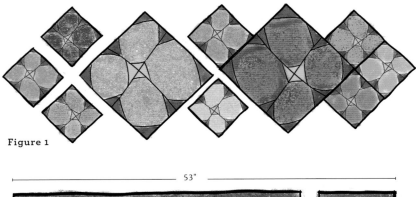

Figure 1

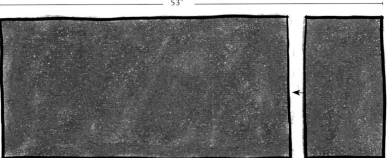

53"

Figure 2

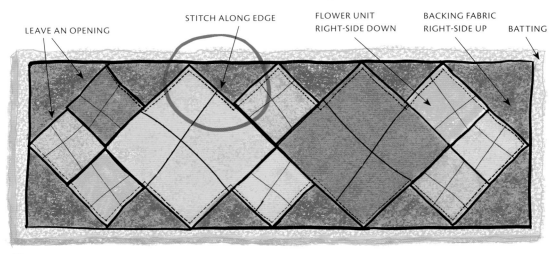

LEAVE AN OPENING

STITCH ALONG EDGE

FLOWER UNIT
RIGHT-SIDE DOWN

BACKING FABRIC
RIGHT-SIDE UP

BATTING

Figure 3

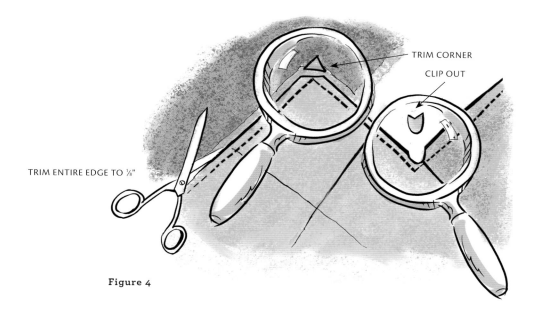

TRIM CORNER

CLIP OUT

TRIM ENTIRE EDGE TO ⅛"

Figure 4

6 Trim the seam allowance, except at the open section, to ⅛" wide. Clip the inner corners in a U shape and the outer corners straight across, very close to the stitching (Figure 4). Be careful not to clip into the stitches.

7 Turn the runner right-side out. Push out the corners well.

8 Press the edges flat. Turn the edges of the opening under and press them so they are even with the sewn edge. Slip stitch the opening closed.

9 Using a matching thread in top and bobbin, topstitch ¼" inside the edge. Keep the needle in the fabric when turning corners.

10 Cut a 25" length of rickrack for each large flower, and a 10" length for each of the small flowers. Curl the rickrack into a spiral, overlapping the cut end at the center of each flower. Sew the rickrack in place with an overcast stitch and matching thread. Hide the other end in a seam by opening one stitch and inserting the end of the rickrack (Figure 5).

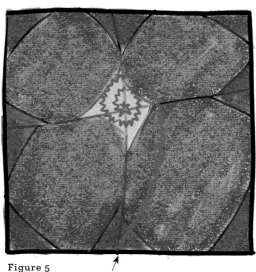

Figure 5

TUCK END IN SEAM

Moonglow Baby Quilt

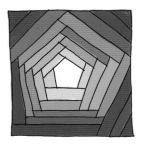

Think of this foundation pieced block as a five-sided Log Cabin block—a house with a peaked roof. For this quilt, ignore the rule about using contrasting values on adjacent pieces. With the graded series of values (see Color Key on next page) you will create the halo around each moon.

Finished quilt: 40" × 40"

Color Key

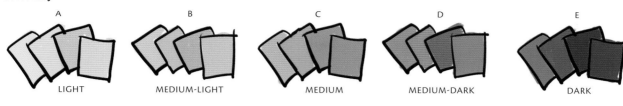

A — LIGHT B — MEDIUM-LIGHT C — MEDIUM D — MEDIUM-DARK E — DARK

Materials, Tools and Cutting Instructions

FOR A SINGLE BLOCK:

* **½ yard or one fat quarter of white fabric** (base fabric/block center)
  - Cut one 13" square.

* **¼ yard (or less) of fifteen to twenty different fabrics.** Choose at least three fabrics of each value from light to dark (see Color Key). The strips may be more than one color, but each group needs to be the same value (see page 20 on discerning values).
  - Cut one 2" wide × approximately 18" long strip from each fabric. You may need to cut more of some values later.

TOOLS:

* Basic cutting and sewing tools

* Pencil

FOR THE BABY QUILT:

* **2 yards of 42"/44" wide prewashed medium-weight white fabric** (base/block center)
  - Cut twelve 7" squares.
  - Cut six 13" squares.

* **Fifteen to twenty fat or long quarters of fabrics in five graded values/colors:** pink to maroon/magenta, light blue to midnight blue, lavender to dark purple, sea foam to dark teal (see Color Key above).
  - Cut approximately half of each value group into 2" strips.

* **⅔ yard of darkest value blue** (inner border, binding)
  - Cut four 1½" × 42"/44" strips (inner border).
  - Cut three 2¼" × 42"/44" strips (binding).

* **⅓ yard of next darkest value fabric** (outer border)
  - Cut four 2½" × 42"/44" strips.

* **1½ yard of fabric** (backing)

* 44" × 44" of thin batting

* Thread to match binding color

* Quilting thread in variegated blues and purples

TOOLS:

* Basic cutting and sewing tools

* Pencil

Make the Wacky Web Block

1 Lightly draw a five-sided shape in the center of the white fabric (like a house with a peaked roof) measuring about 2½"–3" across (Figure 1). The sides may be of different lengths—there's no architect here!

2 Start with a strip of fabric from the lightest value group. Place it right-side down along the inside edge of the pencil line on any side of the "house." Place pins in the strip to mark the beginning and the end of the drawn line. Sew a ¼" seam on the edge aligned with the pencil mark. Only sew between the pins (Figure 2). Do not backstitch.

3 Flip this strip right-side up and finger press. With scissors, trim the ends at angles that continue the adjacent lines (Figure 3). Some of these lines will have odd angles.

4 Moving clockwise, position a different color strip of the lightest value right-side down along the next inside edge of the pencil line. Make sure it covers the end of the first strip and extends beyond the pencil line. Pin, sew, flip and press as in steps 2–3 (Figure 4).

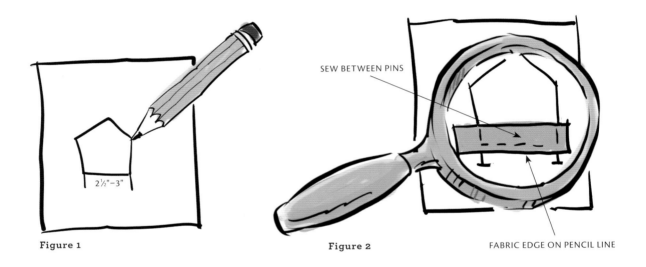

SEW BETWEEN PINS

FABRIC EDGE ON PENCIL LINE

2½"–3"

Figure 1

Figure 2

FLIP, FINGER PRESS AND TRIM

A

Figure 3

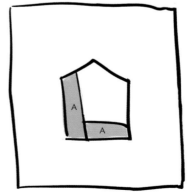

A

A

Figure 4

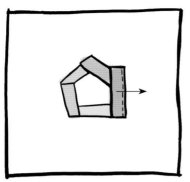

Figure 5

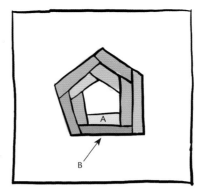

Figure 6

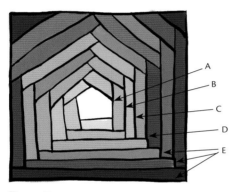

Figure 7

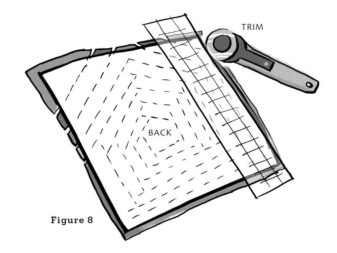

TRIM

BACK

Figure 8

5 Using only the lightest value fabrics, repeat step 4 on the remaining sides of the pentagon. After sewing, flip each strip, press and trim it before placing and sewing the next one (Figure 5). Press or pin to temporarily hold each newly flipped strip flat.

6 When the pentagon has strips sewn completely around it, repeat steps 2–5 using medium-light fabrics on all five sides (Figure 6). After completing each ring, change to the next darker value. When you come to the edges of the block, fill any empty corners with the darkest value fabric (Figure 7).

7 Press the square. Turn it to the back and rotary cut the finished block to measure 12½" square. Extra strip bits hanging over the edge of the base fabric will now get cut off (Figure 8).

Build Your Own Log Cabin

In addition to being one of the easiest blocks to sew, the Log Cabin block is one of the earliest patchwork blocks and one of the most versatile! It can even be made without the foundation fabric on the back. See pages 38–39 for lots of ideas on ways to play with this block.

Make the Moonglow Baby Quilt

1 Following the block instructions, sew six blocks onto 13" white squares. Then trim each to 12½".

2 In the same way, sew twelve blocks onto 7" white squares. (Cut the leftover strips from the large blocks ½" narrower.) Instead of drawing a pentagon in the center of the base, cut a 1½"–2" wide pentagon of light fabric and pin it in the center of each square. As you sew the first ring of darker strips around the pentagon, you will also be stitching down the pentagon. Sew rings around the pentagon as before, using the next darker color value with each ring. Trim excess fabric to the edge of the 7" muslin square.

3 Sew the 7" blocks together in six pairs. Press the seams open. A pair equals half of a large block (Figure 1). Trim each pair to 12½" × 7".

4 Sew the blocks into rows as shown in Figure 2. Press the seams open. Trim as necessary to even up the top and bottom edges of each row.

5 Sew the rows together. Corner matching is not necessary. Press the seams open. Trim the quilt to square.

6 Sew the 1½" inner border strips onto the top and bottom of the quilt. Press and trim off the ends square. Then sew on the top and bottom inner borders (Figure 2). (See "Undercover Stripping" on page 23 for tips on adding borders without stretching them.)

7 Repeat step 6 to sew the 2½" outer border strips to the sides of the quilt.

8 Layer, quilt and bind as instructed on pages 116–121.

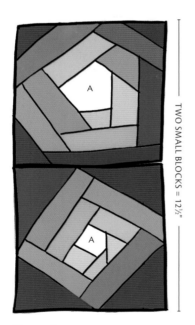

TWO SMALL BLOCKS = 12½"

Figure 1

A Log Cabin By Any Other Color

Make this block look completely different by:

• using scraps without paying attention to the gradations in value.

• reversing the gradations—put the darkest in the center.

• making each side a different color or value.

A Log Cabin By Any Other Shape

Traditionally a Log Cabin block has only four sides. Try it with:

- three, five, six or eight sides. Sides can be equal or unequal lengths. Eight equal sides makes a traditional Pineapple block. Fill the corners to make any of these shapes square.

- different shaped blocks: triangle, rectangle, octagon, diamond or any tessellating shape.

- strips that are tapered instead of perfectly parallel.

- the first piece placed somewhere other than the center—even in a corner.

Figure 2

Cocktail Apron

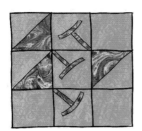

After you've stitched up a batch of these martini blocks, you're on the road to becoming a quiltaholic. Remember: Don't quilt and drive, especially while wearing this cocktail apron!

Materials, Tools and Cutting Instructions

FOR A SINGLE BLOCK:

* **⅓ yard of fabric** (background)
  * Cut nine 4⅝" squares.

* **Three scraps of colorful fabric** (martini glasses)
  * From each, cut a 4⅝" square. Referring to the Cutting Diagram below, cut each square in half once on the diagonal; then cut two 1" wide bias strips from one half of each square. Keep each set together.

* Optional: buttons

TOOLS:

* Basic cutting and sewing tools

* Optional: flannel board (see page 24)

FOR THE COCKTAIL APRON:

* **1½ yards of main fabric** (green background)
  * Cutting parallel to the selvage, cut two 5" × 42"/44" strips (ties, waistband).
  * Cut one 10" × 26" rectangle (apron body).
  * Cut one 3" × 26" strip (lower band).
  * Cut eight 3½" squares (drinks checkerboard).
  * Set aside the remaining fabric (back).

* **¼ yard of second color with similar value** (yellow background)
  * Cut eight 3½" squares (drinks checkerboard).
  * Cut two 1¼" × 26" strips (bands).

* **Variety of colorful/coordinating scraps** (martini glasses)
  * Cut ten 3½" squares. Referring to the Cutting Diagram below, cut each square in half once on the diagonal; then cut two 1" wide bias strips from one half of each square. Keep each set together.

* 11" × 26" of thin batting

* Thread to match main fabric color

* Optional: one 7" square of thin batting (pocket), buttons

TOOLS:

* Basic cutting and sewing tools

* Optional: flannel board (see page 24)

Note: "Swirls" fabric used for these drinks was designed by Joy-Lily for P&B Fabrics in 2006.

Cutting Diagram

Make the Tipsy-Turvy Block

1 Lay out the background squares on a flannel board in three rows of three squares. Arrange the martini glass triangles, each with a stem and base, on top of the background squares.

2 Flip each triangle face down over the opposite side of its square. Position it parallel to the edge of the square, ¼" in from edges. The tips of the triangle will hang over the edge of the background square by just ¼". Sew a ¼" seam along the long edge of the triangle, flip, press (and trim if the triangle hangs over the edge of the background square) (Figure 1). With practice, these will fall exactly into the right place. If they are a tiny bit short of the edge, but not as much as ¼", the seam will cover the shortfall. After sewing, press and return each triangle to its correct position.

3 Press the bias strips lengthwise in thirds (Figure 2). On the shorter strips, also press under the ends.

4 The "stem" (long bias strip) extends from beyond the corner to the mid-point of its square. Topstitch it to the square, leaving the ends raw. Position the "base" piece of bias (short strip) with its center covering the raw edge of the stem. Tug it slightly to create a slight upward or downward curve before stitching it down. Repeat for the other two drinks (Figure 3).

5 Sew the squares into three rows. Sew the rows together, making sure the top ends of the stems are sewn into the seams (Figure 3). Press and trim the block to 12½" square. Garnish drinks with buttons, if you wish.

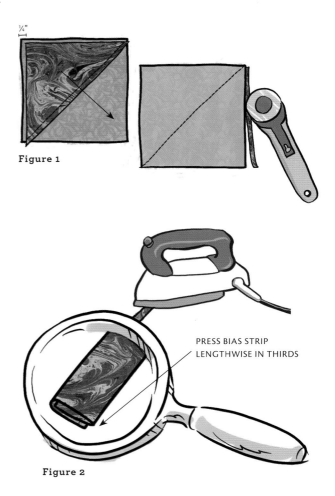

¼"

Figure 1

PRESS BIAS STRIP
LENGTHWISE IN THIRDS

Figure 2

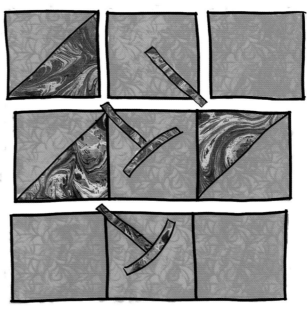

Figure 3

Stem Stuff

Commercial bias tape, rickrack or ribbon could be used for the stem and base of the drinks instead of matching fabric.

Make the Cocktail Apron

1 To make the apron, arrange two rows of eight 3½" squares each on a flannel board, alternating the green and yellow fabric squares. Lay out the drinks triangles with their stems and bases. A few of the stems and bases will hang above or below the main checkerboard (Figure 1).

2 Flip, sew and press each drink triangle and each stem/base to its square, as in steps 2–4 of the block instructions. Once sewn, place the square back in position on the flannel board to avoid getting the pieces mixed up. In the places where it's not possible to finish topstitching the stems and bases, pin them temporarily out of the way on top of their glasses (Figure 2).

3 Sew together each top and bottom pair of squares. Then sew all the pairs together, matching each center seam. Trim the top and bottom edges level as necessary, being careful not to cut off the overhanging stems.

4 Sew 1¼" × 26" bands of yellow fabric to the top and bottom of the checkerboard. Then sew the 3" strip of green to the bottom of the unit (Figure 2). Be sure to catch the stem ends in these seams as necessary. Topstitch the lower stems and bases. Press.

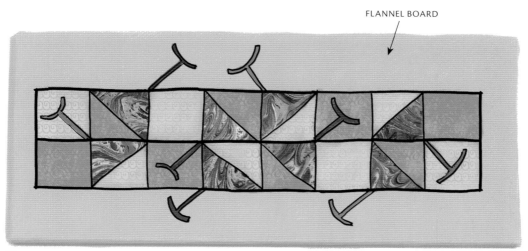

FLANNEL BOARD

Figure 1

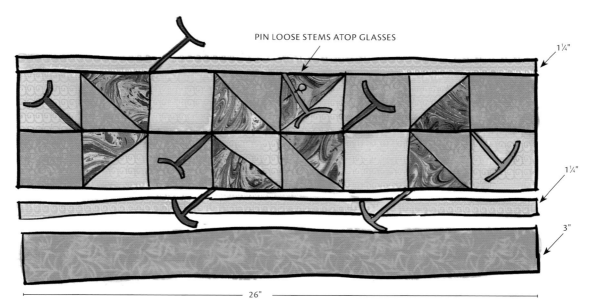

PIN LOOSE STEMS ATOP GLASSES

1¼"

1¼"

3"

26"

Figure 2

5 Lay the checkerboard unit right sides together with the remaining uncut piece of main color backing fabric. Trim the backing to the same size as the checkerboard unit. With the checkerboard and backing still right sides together, lay both pieces on top of the batting, with the checkerboard on top (Figure 3). Place the top edge of the fabrics ¼" above the top edge of the batting. Pin together.

6 Stitch ¼" seam through all three layers on the bottom and both sides. Stop at the end of the batting. Trim the edges of the three sewn sides to ⅛". Clip the corners close to the stitches and turn the rectangle right-side out. Push the corners out well. Fold and press the top edge of the back fabric over the edge of the batting. Don't fold under the raw edge of the checkerboard piece; leave it sticking up.

7 Quilt the rectangle by hand or machine leaving at least 1" unstitched at the top.

8 On the green 10" × 26" main apron body, make narrow hems only on the sides by folding the raw edges ⅛" toward the wrong side of the fabric. Press. Then press under ⅛" again to enclose the raw edges. Stitch these edges using matching green thread in the bobbin.

9 With right sides together, sew the bottom edge of the main apron body to the top raw edge of the checkerboard panel with a ¼" seam. On the back, slip stitch the folded edge to the apron like a hem. Now topstitch the last bases and stems.

10 Adjust the apron waist to the desired size by gathering or pleating along the top edge.

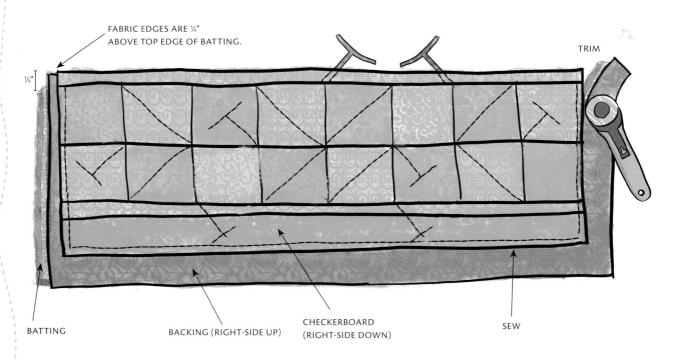

FABRIC EDGES ARE ¼"
ABOVE TOP EDGE OF BATTING.

TRIM

¼"

BATTING

BACKING (RIGHT-SIDE UP)

CHECKERBOARD
(RIGHT-SIDE DOWN)

SEW

Figure 3

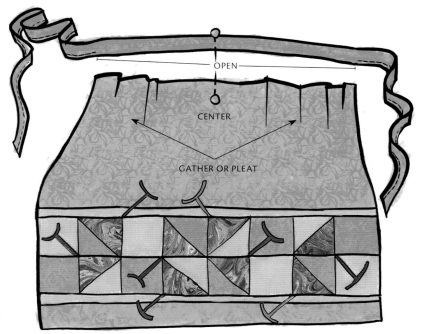

Figure 4

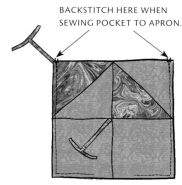

BACKSTITCH HERE WHEN
SEWING POCKET TO APRON.

Figure 5

11 To make the apron ties and waistband, sew the ends of the 5" × 42"/44" strips together, backstitching at the ends of the seam. Press the seam open. Fold and press the strip in half lengthwise, right sides together. Then fold the strip in half width-wise to find the center of the strip, and mark the center with a pin. In the same way, fold and mark the center of the apron top. Match the center of the strip to the center of the apron. With pins, mark where the edges of the skirt meet this strip. Stitch ¼" seam from these "edge of the skirt" pins to the ends of the strip and around the short sides. The center of the strip remains unsewn. Turn the strip right-side out and press the ends of the strip. Press the opening edges under to match the stitched edges (Figure 4).

12 Place the top of the apron ¼" inside the center opening of the strip. Pin together and topstitch along the opening to secure the waistband and close the opening. (You may want to continue topstitching all edges of the ties.)

13 To make a pocket, cut four more 3½" squares from the green fabric and two sets of martini glass fabrics. Lay out the four squares with drinks. Set aside the overhanging stem, and assemble as in block steps 1–3. Place the pocket unit face down on a second fabric for lining. (Use batting too, if desired.) Stitch a ¼" seam around all four sides, leaving a 3" opening on the bottom edge (Figure 5). Clip the corners close to the stitches and turn the pocket right-side out. Push the corners out. Press well, pressing under the raw edges of the opening. Position the pocket on the apron with the opening toward the bottom. Position the remaining stem under the corner of the pocket. Topstitch ⅛" around the sides and bottom. (This also closes the opening.) Backstitch at the top corners of the pocket. Topstitch the overhanging stem and base.

14 Garnish each of the drinks with an interesting button, if you wish.

Wild Goose Chase Wall Quilt

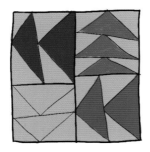

These geese are flying off in all four directions. Some are also flying with no point! They still make a cheerful and easy block or an elegant small quilt.

Finished quilt: 31" × 31"

Materials, Tools and Cutting Instructions

FOR A SINGLE BLOCK:

* **¼ yard fabric** (geese background)
  - Cut nine 4¼" squares. Then cut each square once on the diagonal to make eighteen triangles.

* **¼ yard each of four different fabrics** (geese triangles)
  - Cut four 7" × 7¾" rectangles, each from a different fabric.

TOOLS:

* Basic cutting and sewing tools

FOR THE WALL QUILT:

* **One quarter yard or fat quarter each of three different light colors** (large geese triangles)
  - Cut four 7" × 7¾" rectangles of each color (twelve large geese units).

* **1½ yards of light green fabric*** (four large geese triangles, tiny geese background, borders)
  - Cutting parallel to the selvage, cut two 20" × 5" strips (side borders).
  - Cutting parallel to the selvage, cut two 25" × 5" strips (top and bottom borders).
  - Cutting parallel to the selvage, cut eight 1½" × 20" strips and two 1½" × 6" strips (edges and spacers on border).
  - Cutting parallel to the selvage, cut four 7" × 7¾" rectangles (four large geese units).

Note: If this fabric is so light that dark fabric shows through it (see page 50), reserve 10" × 42"/44" of the light green fabric. Use the optional fusible web and white fabric listed below to line this fabric before cutting the forty 2½" squares below.

  - Cut forty 2½" squares. Cut each square on the diagonal to make eighty triangles (tiny geese background).

* **¼ yard or one fat quarter each of six coordinating colors in medium and dark values** (large geese background, mini-geese triangles)
  - From each color cut eight 4¼" squares. Cut each square on the diagonal and keep triangles of each color together. You may need to cut a few more later (large geese background).
  - From a leftover scrap of each color, cut a 3½" wide strip. Sub-cut each strip into pieces from ½" to 2¼" to make forty small rectangles of assorted colors (tiny geese on the border).

* **½ yard of binding fabric**
  - Cut four strips 2¼" wide.

* 35" × 35" of thin batting

* Thread to match binding color

* Optional: 1¼ yards (18" wide) fusible web, ⅓ yard thin white cotton fabric

TOOLS:

* Basic cutting and sewing tools

* Optional: parchment paper or fusing mat

Make the Wild Geese Block

1 Begin by making the triple goose portion of the block. Working with one 7" × 7¾" rectangle, make two cuts in the 7¾" side at slight angles to make three slightly irregular rectangles (Figure 1).

2 With right sides together, sew a triangle of background fabric to one side of the rectangle so that, when opened, the triangle completely covers the edges of the rectangle (see Flip Tip on the next page). Finger press the seam open (Figure 2). Repeat on the other side of the rectangle (Figure 3). The second triangle may overlap at the center top. The resulting "goose" (the large up-pointing triangle in the middle of the rectangle) may or may not have points or be symmetrical. It's a wild goose! Press.

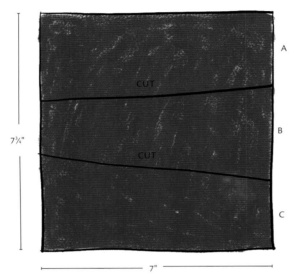

Figure 1

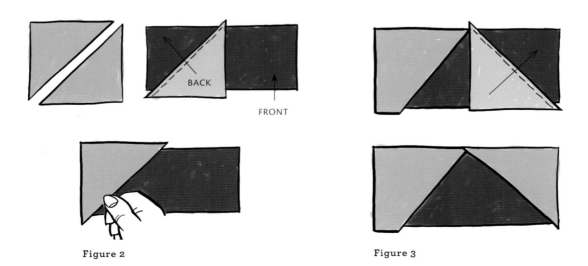

Figure 2   **Figure 3**

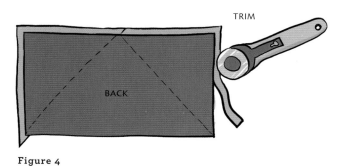

TRIM

BACK

Figure 4

3 From the back side of the goose, trim the overhanging triangle fabric even with the edge of the rectangle (Figure 4).

4 Repeat steps 2–3 with the other two pieces of the same color.

Flip Tip

To make sure that the triangle will cover its corner, press a ¼" fold in the bias edge of the triangle. Place the triangle right-side up covering a corner of the rectangle. Flip the triangle over so it is right-side down. Pin the ¼" fold down to keep the triangle from shifting. Sew on the fold.

PRESS UNDER ¼" FOLD.

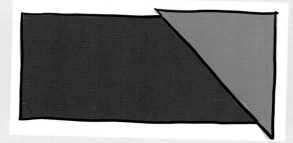

FLIP THE TRIANGLE, PIN AND SEW ALONG FOLD LINE.

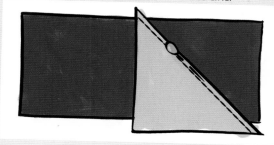

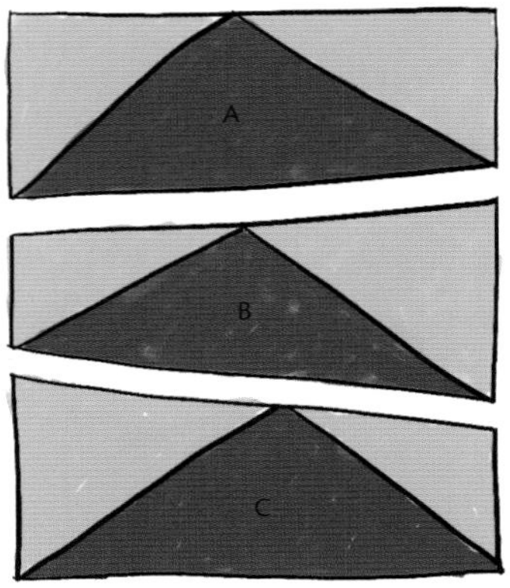

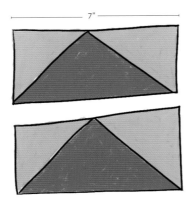

Figure 5 (3-Goose Unit)

7"

Figure 6 (2-Goose Unit)

5 Sew seams to reassemble the three pieces in the same order they were cut (Figure 5). It is alright if some tips disappear in the seams. Trim to 6½" square.

6 To make the double geese portions of the block, trim ½" off the longer side of the rectangles to make them 7" × 7¼". Repeat steps 1–5 with the three 7" × 7¼" rectangles, but this time make only one cut in each rectangle. Reassemble each block of matching color geese by sewing along the cut lines (Figure 6).

7 Arrange these mini-blocks with the geese flying in different directions. Sew pairs together and then join them to complete the block (Figure 7). Trim the completed block to 12½".

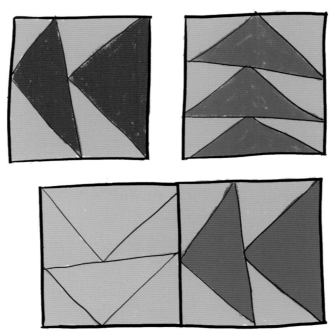

Figure 7

Make the Wild Goose Chase Wall Quilt

1 Make sixteen mini-blocks, as described in steps 1–6 of the block instructions.

Note: The tiny geese on the border have the same values (dark triangle and light background) as the block on page 46. The larger geese on the main part of the quilt are the opposite (light triangle and dark background).

2 Arrange the mini-blocks into four rows of four mini-blocks each with the colors scattered and geese flying in various directions. Sew the mini-blocks together to form rows. Press and trim each row to even the edges. Sew the rows together. Press and trim the quilt edges.

3 Sew approximately forty individual tiny geese, as described in steps 2–4 of the block instructions, using the 3½" wide rectangles and the small light green triangles. Sew nine to eleven geese together into

a strip, all with the points going the same way. Trim the side edges even. Make four geese strips in this way. Sew the 1½" strips of background fabric to the sides of the geese strips. The final trimmed width of one goose strip is 5" (Figure 1). Arrange these strips around the edges of the quilt.

4 Sew a 5" × 20" strip of background fabric to the ends of two tiny-geese strips; sew these strips to the sides of the quilt. Press and trim them even with the quilt. Sew a 5" × 25" strip of background fabric to one end of the remaining two tiny-geese strips. Sew a 1½" × 5" spacer strip of light green fabric to the ends of the longer borders as shown in Figure 2. Sew these strips to the top and bottom of the quilt (Figure 2).

5 Layer, quilt and bind as instructed on pages 116–121.

1½" spacer

Figure 1   **Figure 2**

Zigzag Tote Bag

This block could have been called the Potato Chip block because you can't make just one. Chain sew a quick bagful of 6¹⁄₂" mini-blocks and have fun rotating them—there are several possible arrangements. The ZIGZAG TOTE BAG is big enough to hold your 18" × 24" cutting mat, a big ruler and enough fabric for a bed quilt. Use fewer mini-blocks to make a smaller bag.

Materials, Tools and Cutting Instructions

FOR A SINGLE BLOCK:

* **¼ yard of muslin or white fabric** (base fabric)
  - Cut four 7" squares.

* **¼ yard of dark fabric** (lattice strips)
  - Cut four 10" × 2¼" strips.

* **Assorted 1"–2½" wide strips of scrap fabrics in two value groups: very light and medium-dark**
  (see Color Key on page 35)

TOOLS:

* Basic cutting and sewing tools

FOR THE TOTE BAG:

* **1¼ yards of white fabric** (base fabric)
  - Cut twenty-four 7" squares.

* **¼ yard each of three dark coordinating colors** (lattice strips)
  - Cut eight 10" × 2¼" strips of each dark color (twenty-four strips total).

* **Assorted 1"–2½" wide strips of coordinating fabrics in two value groups: very light and medium-dark**
  - Separate strips by color within each group.

* **1½ yards of 22" wide lightest craft-weight fusible interfacing**
  - Cut two 22" × 24" rectangles.

* **½ yard of non-stretch denim** (bag top and bottom)
  - Cut two 2 × 24½" strips (bag tops).
  - Cut one 4½" × 24½" strip (bag bottom).

* **1 yard of coordinating cotton fabric** (lining)

* **2 yards of handle webbing**

* Navy topstitching thread

TOOLS:

* Basic cutting and sewing tools

* Pencil

* Small ruler

* Fusing mat or parchment paper

* Heavy-duty sewing machine needles (100/16 or 110/18 jeans needles)

Optional: upholstery waterproofing spray

Make the Lattice Alone Block

1 Lay one main lattice strip diagonally right-side up on a 7" base fabric square, centered over the corners (Figure 1).

2 Lay a contrasting color strip from either the dark or light group, long enough to cover the base's edges, right-side down on the lattice strip. Align it with one edge of the lattice strip. Stitch ¼" seam along this edge through all layers. Flip this strip right-side up and finger press (Figure 2).

3 Repeat step 2 with more strips from that value group until the corner is covered. Repeat on the other side of the lattice strip using strips from the other value group. When the entire base fabric is covered with strips, one side will be light and the other dark (Figure 3). Press.

4 From the back, trim the overhanging strips even with the base fabric square (Figure 4).

5 Make three more mini-blocks as in steps 1–4. (Try chain stitching; see page 31.)

6 Arrange the four mini-blocks as desired. Sew the pairs together. Press the seams open. Match the center seams and sew the pairs together to complete the block (Figure 5). (See page 22 for a helpful seam matching technique.) Press the seams open.

7 Trim the block to 12½" square.

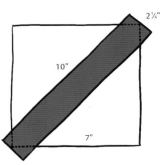

Figure 1

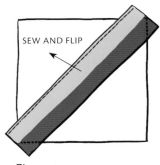

Figure 2

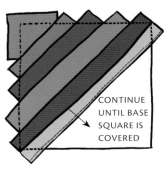

CONTINUE UNTIL BASE SQUARE IS COVERED

Figure 3

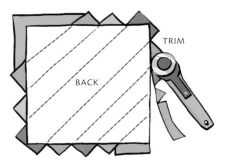

BACK

TRIM

Figure 4

Figure 5

Make the Zigzag Tote Bag

1 Make twenty-four mini-blocks as in steps 1–4 of the block instructions. Sew light-colored strips of a single color group on one side of the main lattice strips, and sew medium-dark strips of a single color group on the opposite side. Trim each block to 6½" square.

2 Lay out twelve mini-blocks in three rows of four blocks each. Use a single color lattice in each row. Rotate the blocks so light strips meet up with light strips in the column adjacent and the row below. Then dark sections will do likewise (Figure 1). The lattice makes a lazy **M** across each row.

3 Sew the blocks together in vertical columns. Press the seams open and replace the blocks in the layout to avoid mixing up pieces.

4 Sew together the columns, matching lattice strips where possible. Press the seams open. Make a second zigzag unit in the same way.

5 Draw a line 2" from the lower cut edge of one 22" × 24" interfacing piece. With the right-side up, place the lower edge of the zigzag unit on this drawn line. Press from the fabric side to fuse the zigzag unit to the interfacing. Use a fusing mat or parchment paper on top to protect the iron (Figure 2). Repeat to fuse the second zigzag unit.

6 Topstitch a simple wavy line pattern across the squares on both units, using a heavy-duty needle on your sewing machine (Figure 3). Continue using this needle for the rest of the bag construction.

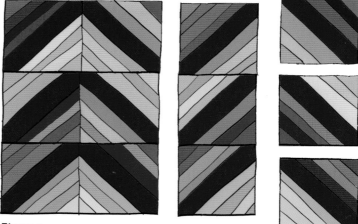

Figure 1

FUSE THROUGH PARCHMENT OR A FUSE MAT

2"

Figure 2

Figure 3

7 Pin a 2" denim strip right-side down along the top edge of each zigzag unit. Stitch ¼" seam through all layers. Flip the denim right-side up, press (and fuse) to the interfacing (Figure 4). Trim fabric to the top of the interfacing.

8 With the right side of both units facing up, overlap the bottom edge of craft interfacing on both units by approximately ½" (Figures 4 and 5). (One M now faces up, the other looks like a W.) Machine stitch close to the edge of the interfacing to join the two pieces. Flip the units over and stitch again close to the other edge of the interfacing. This may require basting to keep the pieces in place while machine stitching.

9 Fold and press under the raw edge of the 4½" denim strip by ¼". Sew the other edge to the bottom of a zigzag unit with ¼" seam, front sides together. Fuse the denim strip to the interfacing with the folded edge overlapping the edge of the lattice squares. Topstitch close to the fold to secure the denim in place. Topstitch the other edge to match.

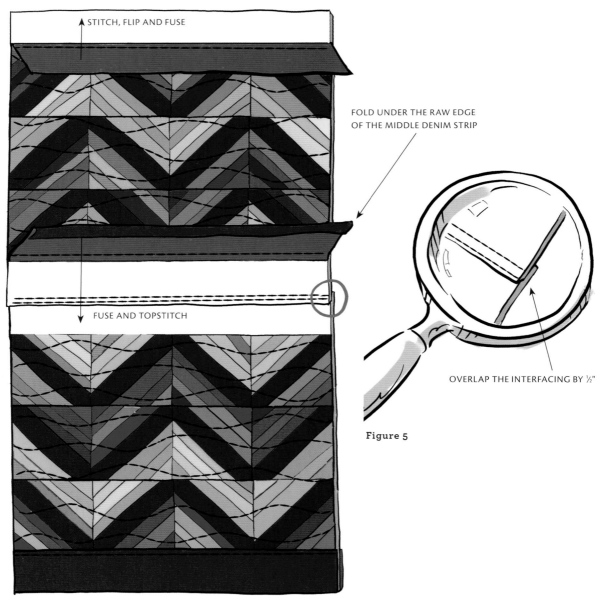

STITCH, FLIP AND FUSE

FOLD UNDER THE RAW EDGE OF THE MIDDLE DENIM STRIP

FUSE AND TOPSTITCH

OVERLAP THE INTERFACING BY ½"

Figure 5

Figure 4

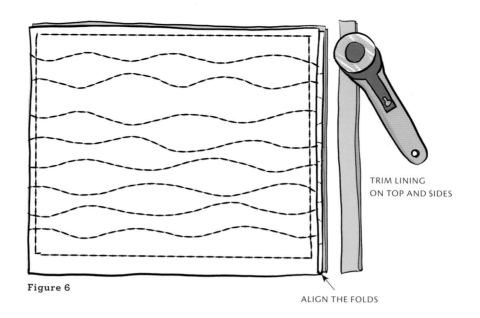

TRIM LINING
ON TOP AND SIDES

ALIGN THE FOLDS

Figure 6

10 Fold the bag in half, right sides together. Match the denim seams, and then align the other seams as best as you can. Sew along both sides with ³⁄₈" seam allowance.

11 Fold the lining fabric in half with right sides together. (You may need to add a piece of fabric to make the lining as big as the bag.) Lay the bag on top of the lining, aligning the bottom folds. Cut the folded lining piece along the top and sides so it is exactly the size of the folded bag (Figure 6).

12 Keeping the sides of the lining and the bag aligned, slide the bag 1"–2" below the top of the lining. With a small ruler, draw a short pencil line extending from the bag's side stitching to the top edge of the lining (Figure 7). (Start the lining seams exactly at these marks so the sizes of the bag and lining openings will be equal.)

13 Separate the bag and lining. Pin the lining as it is folded, and sew starting directly on the pencil lines. Leave a side opening of at least 14" in the center of one side.

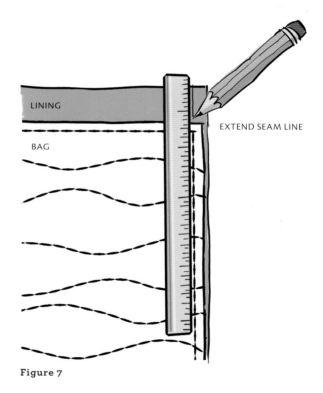

LINING

BAG

EXTEND SEAM LINE

Figure 7

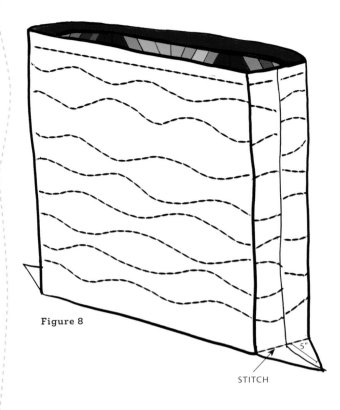

Figure 8

STITCH

5"

14 With the bag still inside out, make bottom corners: Flatten the bottom 5" of the side seam into a triangle (measure 5" from the tip of the triangle along the seam). Adjust the triangle equally on both sides of the seam. Stitch across the triangle perpendicular to the seam (Figure 8). Repeat on the other side and also on both sides of the lining. Turn the bag right-side out.

15 Cut the webbing for the straps in half. Pin one piece of webbing to the bag, centering the handles. Leave 1" of webbing sticking above the top and the rest hanging down. Try it on your shoulder and adjust the strap length. Pin the other handle at a matching length and location. Be sure the handles are not twisted. Stitch $\frac{1}{8}$" from the top edge of the bag to attach the handles and backstitch to secure (Figure 9).

STITCH HANDLES

Figure 9

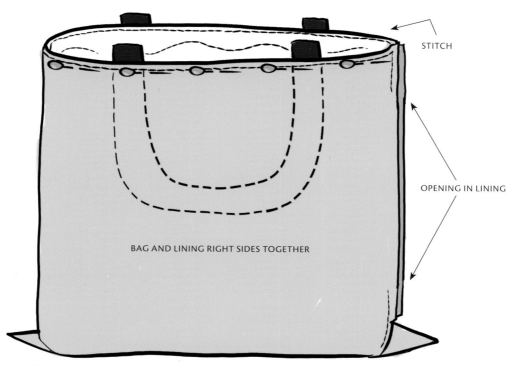

STITCH

OPENING IN LINING

BAG AND LINING RIGHT SIDES TOGETHER

Figure 10

16 Slide the inside-out lining over the bag (with the handles still hanging downward). Align the bag and lining side seams at the top edge. Pin all around the top opening. Stitch with ¼" seam around the top (Figure 10). This seam is deeper than the stitches securing the handles, so those stitches will now vanish.

17 Reach through the opening in the lining and pull the bag through it.

18 Sew the lining opening closed by hand or machine. Push the lining down into bag.

19 Press out the seam flush at the edge. Topstitch along the top edge of the bag to secure the lining (Figure 11). If the interfacing is fusible on both sides, you can also fuse the lining to the interfacing.

Note: For heavy-duty use, you may want to spray the outside of your bag with an upholstery waterproofing spray.

PRESS AND TOPSTITCH

Figure 11

Stack, Slice, Swap and Sew Blocks

These blocks are very fast and easy to make—perfect for beginning quilters! Each is made in pairs of two, except for the Four Play pattern which makes four blocks at a time. To make these instantly gratifying blocks, you will cut two fabrics simultaneously and then swap the same parts between the two fabrics. Remember to always start cutting with both fabrics facing up.

Each time you sew together two fabrics using a ¼" seam, you will lose ½" from the final size of the piece. That's why each of these blocks starts with a 14" or 15" square; you will still end up with a finished block big enough to trim to a 12½" square.

A flannel board is a really handy tool for keeping your pieces in the correct position before and after sewing each section. Instructions for making a flannel board are on page 24.

Square Dance Quilt

This block is created in groups of four blocks at once, and making four is almost as fast as making a single block! If you need to make a baby quilt in a hurry, make three sets of these blocks, and your quilt will come together as fast as contractions.

Finished quilt: 49" × 50"

Materials, Tools and Cutting Instructions

FOR FOUR BLOCKS:

✳ **One fat quarter or ½ yard each of two contrasting fabrics**

- Stack the two fabrics right-side up.

- Cut a 14½" square from both fabrics at once. Leave the squares perfectly stacked.

✳ **Two large scraps of accent fabric**

- Cut two 5½" squares.

✳ **½ yard of white-on-white print fabric**

- See cutting directions in step 7.

TOOLS:

✳ Basic cutting and sewing tools

✳ Optional: flannel board (see page 24)

FOR THE QUILT:

✳ **1 yard each of two contrasting fabrics**

- Stack the two contrasting fabrics, both right-side up.

- Cut four 14½" squares from both fabrics at once (for a total of eight squares). Leave the squares stacked as cut.

✳ **⅓ yard total of accent colors or assorted scraps**

- Cut eight 5½" squares.

✳ **2 yards of white-on-white print or other background color fabric**

- See cutting directions in step 7.

✳ 53" × 54" batting

✳ Thread to match background color

✳ **½ yard of fabric or leftover fabric** (binding)

- Cut six 2¼" × 42"/44" strips. Or, if using leftover fabric, assemble 2¼" strips to make a total length of 200".

TOOLS:

✳ Basic cutting and sewing tools

✳ Optional: flannel board (see page 24)

Make the Four Play Block

1 Place two accent squares right-side up in the middle of the large squares (also right-side up).

2 Using a ruler and rotary cutter, make two slightly angled vertical cuts just inside the edge of the accent fabrics (Figure 1). Rotate the ruler 90 degrees and repeat to make horizontal cuts. This creates a grid of nine irregular squarish shapes. Lift the accent pieces and remove the two pieces of main fabric below them. Put the accent fabrics in their place (Figure 2).

3 Swap the top and bottom fabrics on each of the four corners to create a checkerboard (Figure 3).

SWAP LAYERS ON FOUR CORNERS

Figure 3

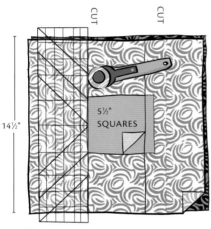

Figure 1

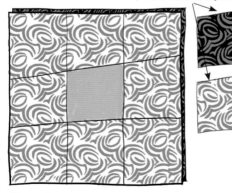

REMOVE BOTTOM
TWO CENTER SQUARES

Figure 2

Four Play Mini-Block

To make a mini-block, begin with two 9" main squares and two 3½" accent squares. You will wind up with four mini-blocks that you will trim to 6½" square. These can be used in border designs or assembled into a single 12½" block, like the one in the sampler quilt on page 108.

FLANNEL BOARD

Figure 4

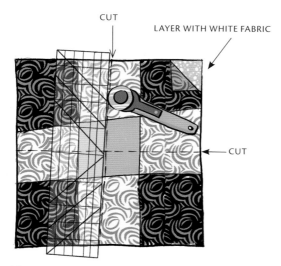

CUT

LAYER WITH WHITE FABRIC

CUT

Figure 5

4 Place one layer of pieces carefully in order on a flannel board or other nonslip surface to keep them in position while working on the other set (Figure 4). Keep all the pieces in the correct locations or risk madness!

5 Using a ¼" seam allowance, sew one set of pieces together into rows. Press the seams. Sew the three rows together, matching seams when possible.

6 Repeat step 5 with the other set of pieces. You now have two warped Nine Patch squares. Press.

7 Put one Nine Patch on top of the white-on-white fabric, both right-side up. Trim the white fabric to match the Nine Patch square. With the two squares still stacked, rotary cut through the middle of both layers, top to bottom and side to side. Make the cuts as off-centered and angled as desired (Figure 5).

8 Swap layers in the top-left and bottom-right positions. Lay one set on the flannel board. Sew together each pair of pieces, and then sew the two units together for each block. Match the center seam. Each Nine Patch makes two blocks (Figure 6).

9 Repeat step 8 with the other Nine Patch.

10 Press. Trim each block to 12½" square.

ONE NINE-PATCH MAKES TWO BLOCKS.

Figure 6

Make the Square Dance Quilt

1 Following steps 1–10 of the block instructions, make four sets of four blocks (sixteen blocks total).

2 Lay out the individual blocks in four rows of four blocks each in a pleasing arrangement. There are many possibilities (see illustrations at right for two possible layouts). Assemble the blocks in rows, and then sew the rows together to complete the quilt top.

3 Layer, quilt and bind as instructed on pages 116–121.

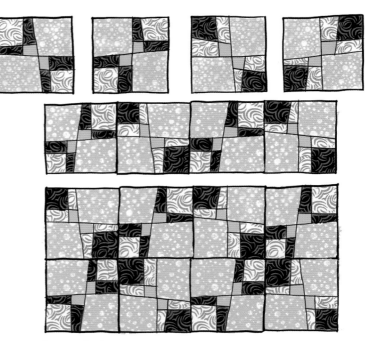

Layout Option 1

Layout Option 2

Four Play Blocks Become Diagonal Stripes

This block lends itself to lots of different layouts and arrangements. Play with the layout of your quilt and take digital photos of each design. That way, you can look over the layouts, choose the one you like the best and easily re-create it with the help of the photo. You can also use more than one background fabric. I used one white-on-white print in the SQUARE DANCE QUILT, but this quilt uses black and white fabrics in step 6.

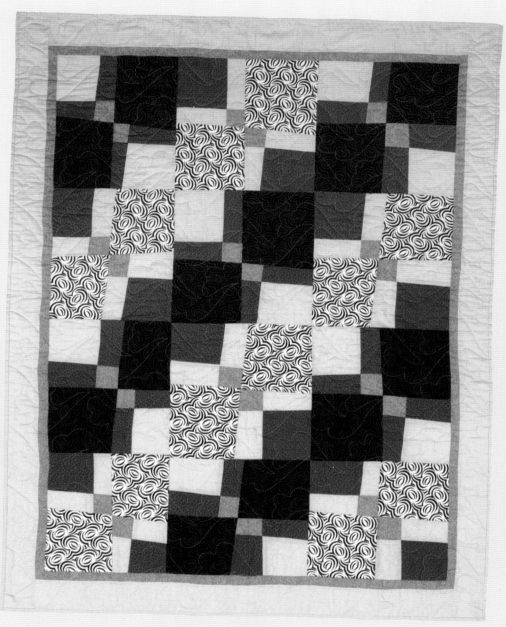

GEE WHIZ WEDGE BLOCKS
Crayons Quilt

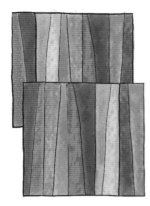

This block was inspired by a particular Gee's Bend quilt made of string-pieced columns by Jessie T. Pettway. It's definitely carefree and rule-breaking!

As a child, I organized my crayons by color in shoeboxes with cardboard divisions for different colors. It was probably the beginning of my love and study of color. The multicolored bars in this quilt remind me those boxes, so I appliquéd crayons on the extra-wide border. Flowers or other appliqué motifs would look great, too.

Finished quilt: 59" × 74"

Materials, Tools and Cutting Instructions

FOR TWO BLOCKS:

✴ **Ten coordinating/contrasting fat quarters or long quarters** (wedges)

- Group the ten fabrics into five pairs, each fabric paired with a contrasting fabric.
- Stack the first contrasting pair of fabrics, both right-side up. Cut one 4" × 13½" strip from the stack.
- Stack three more pairs of fabrics in the same way. From each of these stacks, cut one 3½" × 13½" strip.
- Stack the fifth pair of fabrics in the same way. From this stack, cut one 2¾" × 13" strip.
- Keep each pair together.

TOOLS:

✴ Basic cutting and sewing tools

FOR THE QUILT:

✴ **Twelve fat quarters in medium-light, medium and medium-dark values** (see page 20 on discerning values) (wedges, crayons)

- Layer two stacks of six fabrics each, all face-up. From both of the stacks, cut three 3" × 13½" strips, two 2½" × 13½" strips and one 4" × 13½" strip, for a total of seventy-two strips. You may need to cut more as you go along (wedges).
- Set aside the scraps (crayons).

✴ **⅓ yard each of three colorful fabrics** (inner borders)

- From each color, cut four 2" strips to total 150" of length.

✴ **2¾ yards of dark background fabric** (outer borders, column spacers, binding)

- See cutting directions in step 8.

✴ Approximately 63" × 78" of thin batting (Quilt sizes will vary based on column width and length; measure finished quilt top and add about 3" all around to determine batting size.)

✴ Thread to match border color

TOOLS:

✴ Basic cutting and sewing tools

✴ Paper-cutting knife or small rotary cutter

✴ File folder for template

✴ Pencil

✴ Another long quilters ruler

✴ Optional: travel or appliqué iron, tweezers

Make the Gee Whiz Wedge Blocks

1 From each of the five stacked strip pairs, make a diagonal cut 1" in from the top left corner and 1" in from the bottom right corner; the right sides of both fabrics should be up (Figure 1). Swap the fabric layers on one side of the cut.

2 Pin together each contrasting pair. Using ¼" seam allowance, sew along the diagonal cuts (Figure 2). Press all ten pieces.

3 Using one pair of each color group, lay out five rectangles into a pleasing arrangement. Keep the narrowest strips away from the edge, because they could get trimmed into oblivion. Sew the pieced rectangles together and press.

4 Trim the block to 12½" square.

5 Repeat steps 3–4 with the other set of rectangles, perhaps arranging them in a different order.

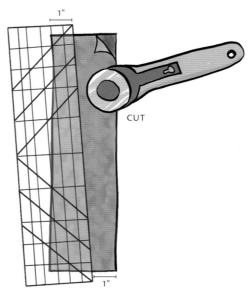

1"

CUT

1"

Figure 1

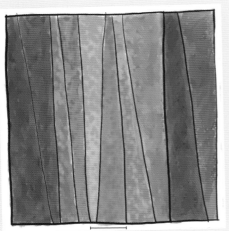

Variation

When cutting the pieced rectangles, it is fine to occasionally reverse the cuts of the angles for variety.

REVERSED
SECTION

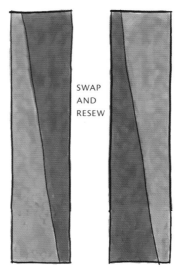

SWAP
AND
RESEW

Figure 2

Pressing Tip

Pressing may cause diagonal seams to curve. To correct this, firmly pull one end of the fabric straight while pressing the seam with jets of steam.

Make the Crayons Quilt

1 Pair up strips of the same width into contrasting sets. Cut on the diagonal, swap and sew each of these sets into two wedge units as described in steps 1–2 of the block instructions.

2 Arrange the pieced rectangles in a pleasing order in two 58"–60" long columns (Figure 1). To sew the long columns of wedges into a single bar, start by sewing groups of 6–8 pieced rectangles together. Press and stretch the segment (see pressing tips on page 70 and below). Then sew these segments together until the necessary length is achieved. Making 12" blocks is not necessary.

3 Trim the sides of both columns to clean up the edges. The columns may be 11½"–12½" wide after trimming; make sure they are the same width, top and bottom.

4 For the narrow center bar, repeat steps 1–2, making several wedge segments that total approximately 32". Before sewing the segments together, cut each segment in half perpendicular to the seams and reorganize them into one tall column (Figure 2). Sew the segments together, press and trim as in steps 2–3. The center column may be 6"–6½" wide after trimming.

5 Sew together the 2"-wide strips of each inner border fabric into two long strips per color. Backstitch at the beginning and end of these joining seams and press them open.

APPROX. 12"

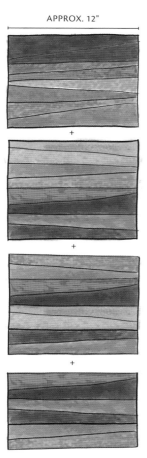

Figure 1

6½"

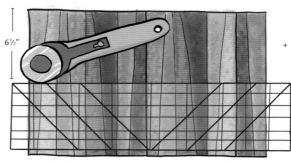

Figure 2

Triple Press

With so many seams, these segments will be very elastic. To flatten them completely, first press on the back with all the seams going in one direction. Then press on the front to flatten out any folds. Finally, press on the front once more, using jets of steam while stretching the fabric with your free hand.

6 Using one color per column, sew the 2" inner border strips onto the long sides of all three wedge columns with a ¼" seam allowance (Figure 3). Pin the strip right sides together to one side of the column, and sew with the strip next to the feed dogs of your machine. As you sew, gently pull on the wedges; this helps prevent rippling. At the end of the column, cut off the remaining strip and set it aside for the short ends.

7 Trim all three columns to the same length. Mine are 56" long, but yours don't need to be exactly that size, just equal. Sew strips of the matching color on the short ends of each column.

8 Measure the length of a column and add 4". Cut this length from the dark background yardage. Set the rest aside. From this length, parallel to the selvage, cut two strips 5" wide for column spacers and four strips 7½" wide for borders. Cut seven 2¼"-wide strips for binding. From the leftover yardage, cut a 32" × 7½" strip; sub-cut this strip into four 8" × 7½" sections for piecing the longer borders.

9 Using a ¼" seam allowance, sew the pieced columns, background spacers and side borders together. Trim the top and bottom edges. Attach additional 8" strips to extend the top and bottom borders. Then sew borders to the quilt. Trim edges (Figure 3).

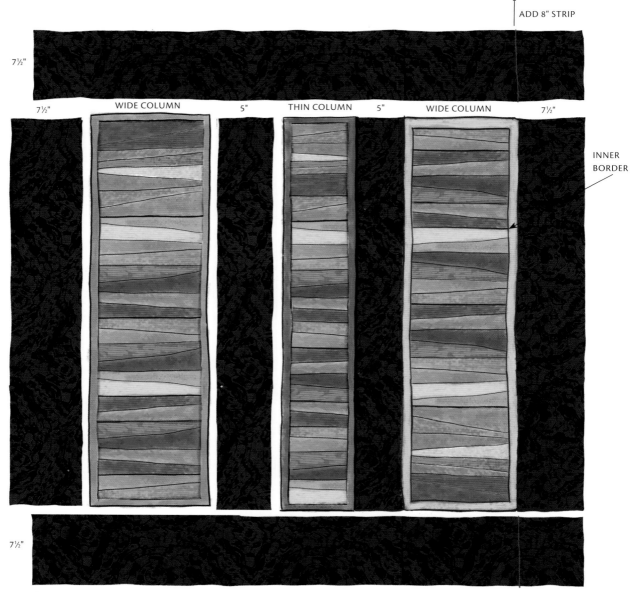

Figure 3

10 Using a pencil and ruler, draw a simplified crayon shape 5½" high and ¾" wide on a file folder. Cut the shape out carefully with a ruler and sharp paper knife or a small-blade rotary cutter. (Scissors do not make a straight enough cut.)

11 Lay the crayon pattern on the wrong side of a leftover scrap of wedge fabric. Cut the fabric roughly ¼" larger than the pattern. Press the fabric edges over the pattern (Figure 4). Try using a smaller iron or tweezers to protect your fingers. The crayon tips may be folded bluntly—it's easier and more realistic than sharp points. Remove and reuse the crayon pattern. Cut and press about twenty-four crayons in assorted colors.

12 Position the fabric crayons with folded edges down, scattered on the borders. Stitch them down by hand or machine.

13 Trim the quilt edges straight and square (see tips below). Layer, quilt and bind as explained on pages 116–121.

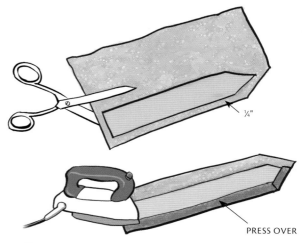

¼"

PRESS OVER

Figure 4

The Ins and Outs of Trimming a Border Wider Than Your Ruler

Use two long quilting rulers to trim the edges of a large quilt with wide borders. Line up one ruler—the outer ruler—in the middle of a cut edge of the quilt. Line up the second ruler—the inner ruler—just below it on the quilt. Keep both ruler edges firmly touching through this whole process. Notice where a line on the inner ruler aligns to an inner horizontal seam. Keeping the seam on this line, slide the inner ruler to the left, about halfway past the end of the outer ruler. Then slide the outer ruler half a length to the left. Continue sliding the rulers alternately, to the left edge. Repeat to the right edge. Trim along the top edge of the outer ruler. This is a good time to practice the carpenters' credo, "Measure twice and cut once." Trim all four edges in this manner. If the quilt is not exactly square it will still appear square if the borders are parallel with the design.

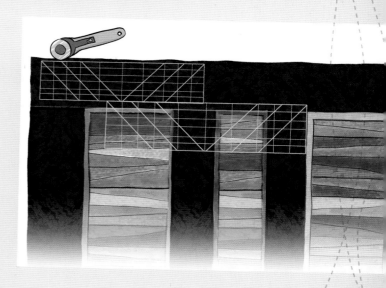

Garden Path Quilt

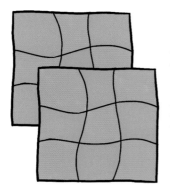

Some quilters will stitch miles of appliqué to avoid sewing curved seams. By the time you have made a pair of these curvy Nine Patch blocks, you will be an expert at curved seams because they are actually quite easy to sew! The GARDEN PATH QUILT shows off a very large scale, beautiful print fabric by "fussy cutting" whole blocks. You will definitely want a $12^{1}/_{2}$" square ruler to do this. Quilting doesn't get much easier, so for a little challenge, all the blocks are set "on point," or tilted at 45-degree angles (see page 113).

Finished quilt: 48" × 63"

Materials, Tools and Cutting Instructions

FOR TWO BLOCKS:

✳ **Two fat quarters of contrasting fabrics**

- Stack the two fabrics right-side up.
- Cut a 14" square from both fabrics at once. Leave the squares perfectly stacked.

TOOLS:

✳ Basic cutting and sewing tools

✳ Pencil

✳ Optional: paper scissors, file folder for template, paper scissors flannel board (see page 24)

FOR THE QUILT:

✳ **1⅝ yards of lime green main accent color fabric** (Nine Patches, inner border, binding)

- Cutting parallel to the selvage, cut four 1½" wide strips (inner border).
- Cutting parallel to the selvage, cut five 2¼" wide strips (binding).
- Cut two 14" × 14" squares.

✳ **½ yard of light yellow fabric**

- Cut two 14" × 14" squares.

✳ **One fat quarter each of gold and melon colors**

- Cut one 14" × 14" square from each color.

✳ **Large print fabric**: 2 yards if using a very large-print fabric with a distinct "up and down" pattern, or 1½ yards if using a smaller print or one without a distinct direction (fussy-cut blocks, border cornerstones, setting triangles)

- See cutting directions in steps 2–4.

✳ **1⁵/₈ yards complementary fabric** (border)

- Cutting parallel to the selvage, cut two 6½" × 38" strips and two 6½" × 56" strips.

✳ 52" × 67" of thin batting

✳ Thread to match binding color

TOOLS:

✳ Basic cutting and sewing tools

✳ Pencil

✳ 12½" square plastic ruler

✳ Optional: paper scissors, file folder for template, paper scissors flannel board (see page 24)

Make the Curvy Nine Patch Blocks

1 Mark 4¼" in from each corner with a pencil. Draw a gently curved line between the top and bottom marks. To avoid "dog ears," the curved line should begin and end perpendicular to the edge of the fabric. (Make a file folder template for the curves if you prefer.) Rotary cut along the two drawn curves from the bottom to the top of the square through both layers (Figure 1).

2 Swap the top and bottom layers of the middle section. Lay out the pieces of both layers in position on a flannel board (Figure 2).

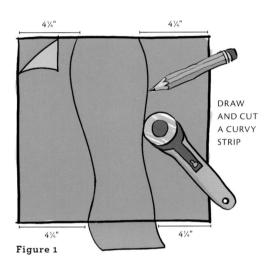

4¼"   4¼"

4¼"   4¼"

DRAW AND CUT A CURVY STRIP

Figure 1

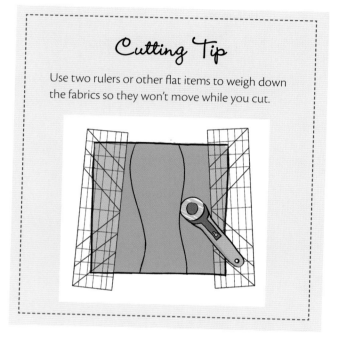

Cutting Tip

Use two rulers or other flat items to weigh down the fabrics so they won't move while you cut.

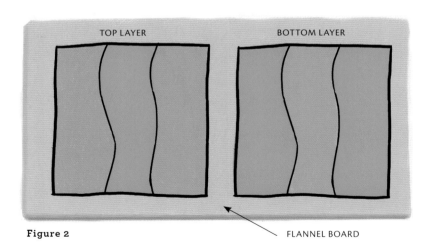

TOP LAYER   BOTTOM LAYER

Figure 2   FLANNEL BOARD

Curvy Nine Patch Mini-Block

Begin with 8" squares instead of 14" squares. Follow steps 1–6, cutting very slight curves. In step 2, mark 2¾" in from the corners instead of 4¼". Trim the finished blocks to 6½" squares.

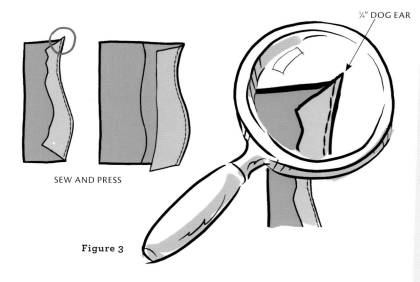

¼" DOG EAR

SEW AND PRESS

Figure 3

Easy Curves Ahead

To sew curved seams like a pro, line up the tops and cut edges of the curved pieces, right sides together. If one piece has a steep angle at the top, raise its tip ¼" above the other piece; this is called a *dog ear* (Figure 3). Begin sewing right where the two pieces cross. Gently guide the two edges together as you sew a scant ¼" seam. Stop often with the needle down to realign the edges and to move extra fabric away from the needle. You will be surprised how easy it is to sew shallow curves like these.

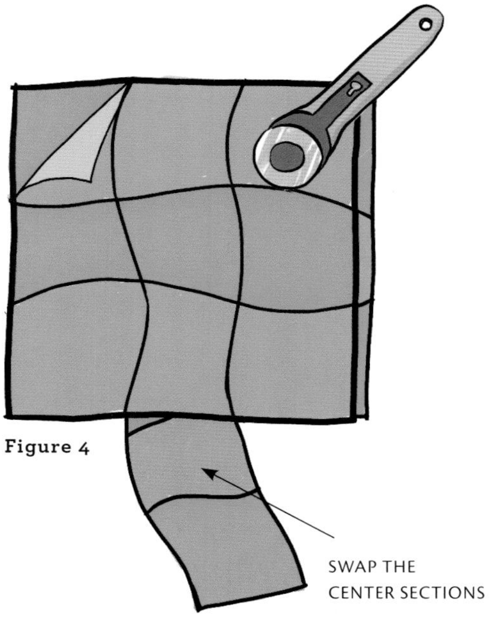

Figure 4

SWAP THE
CENTER SECTIONS

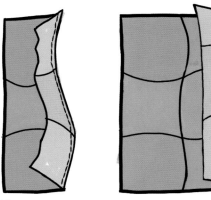

Figure 5

3 Using a scant ¼" seam allowance, sew the curved pieces together to reassemble each layer (Figure 3).

4 On one layer, press the curved seams toward the center. On the other, press toward the outside edges.

5 Place one layer exactly on top of the other, both right-side up with seams aligned. Lay the fabric stack on a cutting board with the center stripe horizontal. Cut as in step 1, at 90 degrees to the first cuts (Figure 4).

6 Switch the middle strips, lay out each layer in position, and sew each layer back together as in step 3, matching corners and seams where possible (Figure 5).

7 Press the seams. Trim each block to 12½" square.

Make the Garden Path Quilt

1 Following steps 1–7 of the block instructions, make three pairs of blocks, pairing colors as shown in the quilt photo on page 74. Press and trim all blocks to 12½" square for a total of six Curvy Nine Patches.

2 From the large-print fabric, fussy cut two 12½" squares (A) with your favorite cropping of the fabric's design. Preview the cuts with a square ruler (Figure 1). These blocks may be cut straight on the grain or at a 45-degree diagonal (Figure 2).

3 From the large-print fabric, cut one 18½" square. Cut it on both diagonals into four triangles (B). Then cut two more triangles this size with the long side of the triangle parallel to the selvage (Figure 2).

Note: If the printed fabric has a specific up and down, mark left, right, top and bottom triangles. The extra two triangles should be left- and right-side orientation on the print.

4 From the large-print fabric, cut two 13½" squares (C). Cut both squares in half on the diagonal. (If there is a specific up and down pattern, cut one square from top left to bottom right. Cut the other from top right to bottom left.) Mark the pieces as shown. Fussy cut four 5½" squares (D) for the border cornerstones (Figure 2).

5 Lay out the blocks and triangles according to the diagram (Figure 3). Smaller triangles go in the corners. Be sure to orient any up-down patterns of the fabric in the correct direction.

6 Pin each diagonal row of blocks and triangles together. Pin at 1" intervals to stop bias from stretching. With bias-cut fabric on the bottom, sew the blocks together in rows. Don't sew over pins; pull them out at the last second before the machine gets to them (Figure 4).

7 To sew rows together, start pinning at the center seam. Match corners of blocks (see page 22) and pin extensively. Sew all rows together. Press and trim the edges of the quilt straight.

FUSSY CUT TWO 12½" SQUARES.

Figure 1

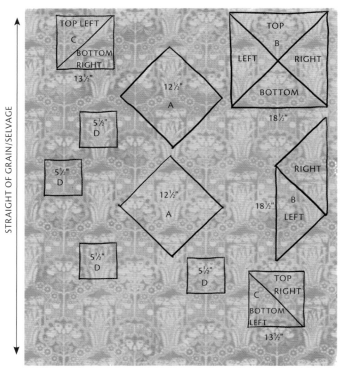

Figure 2

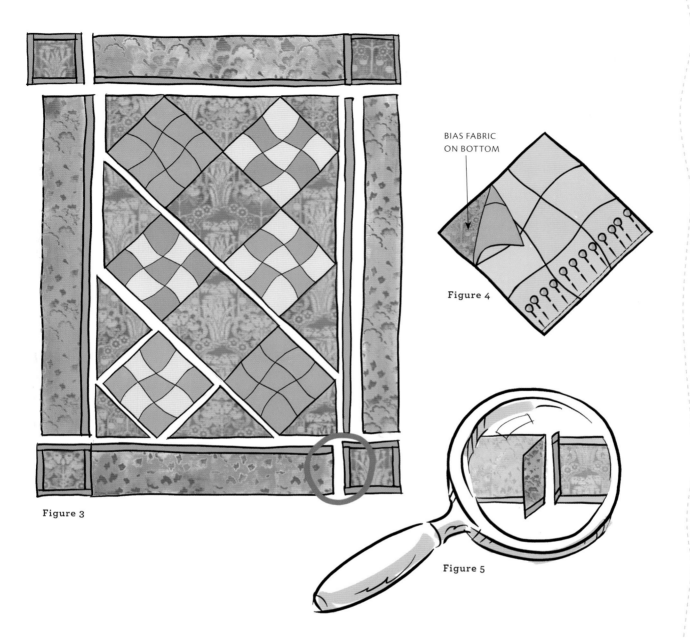

BIAS FABRIC
ON BOTTOM

Figure 4

Figure 3

Figure 5

8 Sew the 1½"-wide inner border strips to the 6½"-wide border strips. Trim ends.

9 Sew the 1½"-wide inner border strips to all sides of the 5½" squares you cut in step 4. These are *cornerstones.*

10 Sew the two longer borders to sides of the quilt. Sew with the main quilt on top and the border strip next to the feed dogs of your machine. (See page 23 for more information.) Press seams and trim the edges even with the top and bottom of the quilt.

11 Sew a cornerstone to one end of each remaining border piece.

12 Line up the green strip on the cornerstone with the green strip on the main border. (See page 22 for a seam alignment tip.) Sew this border to the bottom of the quilt, stopping a few inches before the end of the main border strip. To attach the last cornerstones, remove the quilt from the machine. Press a 90-degree fold in the border where it aligns with the main quilt. Press a ¼" fold on the adjacent side of the cornerstone. With right sides together, match up the folds (Figure 5). Sew on the fold line. Then finish sewing the main seam. Repeat with the remaining border and last cornerstone. Press the quilt.

13 Trim the quilt edges straight and square. Layer, quilt and bind as explained on pages 116–121.

Reversible Place Mats

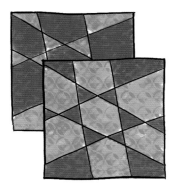

One day as I was slicing and swapping fabric for fun, a six-pointed star appeared! Sew up a pair of place mats pronto with this pointy-headed technique. (The block is still 12½" square, but I've made some adjustments for the place mats to make them a better size.)

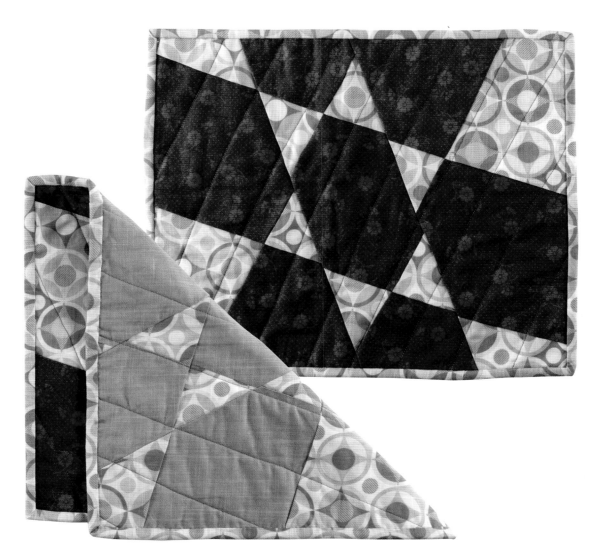

Finished place mat: 13" × 16"

Materials, Tools and Cutting Instructions

FOR TWO BLOCKS:

✳ **Two fat quarters of coordinating fabrics**

- Stack the fat quarters, both right-side up.
- Cut a 14" × 15" rectangle from both fabrics at once. Keep the fabrics stacked as cut.

TOOLS:

✳ Basic cutting and sewing tools

✳ Fabric marking pencil

FOR TWO PLACE MATS:

✳ **½ yard each of two coordinating fabrics, or four coordinating fat quarters**

- Stack two contrasting fabrics, both right-side up. Cut a 14" × 18" rectangle from both fabrics at once. Keep the layers stacked as cut.
- Cut another pair of 14" × 18" rectangles. (They may be the same color or two different colors.)

✳ 14" × 36" of thin batting

✳ **¼ yard of coordinating fabric** (binding)

- Cut three 2¼" wide strips.

✳ Thread to complement fabrics

TOOLS:

✳ Basic cutting and sewing tools

✳ Fabric marking pencil

Make the Jaunty Star Blocks

1 With the two 14" × 15" rectangles stacked horizontally, mark 2¼" in from the top left corner along the 15" side. Then mark 2¼" in from the bottom right corner. Using a ruler and rotary cutter, cut a 4½"-wide diagonal strip with these marks as outer edges (Figure 1).

2 Switch the top and bottom center strips. Using ¼" seam allowance, sew the top layer together. Sew the lower layer together (Figure 2). Press the seams toward the darker fabric.

3 Restack the two layers right-side up with the seams aligned. Rotate the stack 90 degrees to the left. Repeat steps 1–2, this time marking 3" in from the top left and bottom right corners. Cut a 4½" diagonal strip with these marks as outer edges as before (Figure 3).

RESEW LAYERS

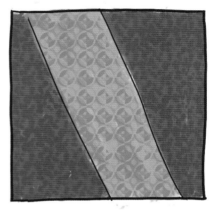

Figure 2

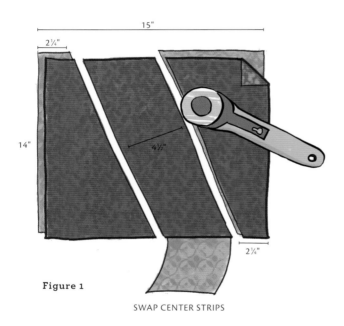

Figure 1

SWAP CENTER STRIPS

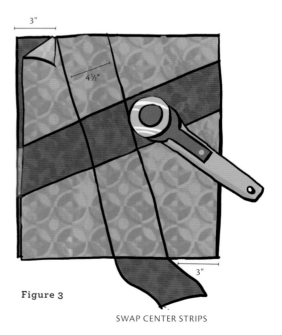

Figure 3

SWAP CENTER STRIPS

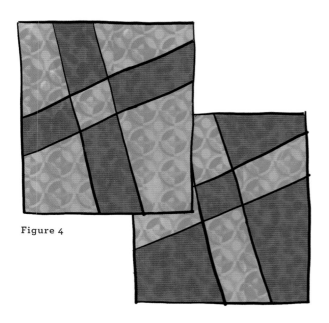

Figure 4

4 Switch the top and bottom center strips (Figure 3). Sew the top layer together. Sew the bottom layer together (Figure 4). Press the seams.

5 Restack the two layers right-side up with the seams aligned as closely as possible. Cut a center strip approximately 4" wide through both pieces together. Before cutting, stand the ruler on edge to preview where the cut might go. Check both sides of the ruler's edge to see that the small triangles formed on both sides of each cut will all be about equal sizes (Figure 5). This is more important than whether the cuts are parallel.

6 Swap the middle sections and pin seams starting in the center to get seams as close as possible. Sew the layers together as before, using only ⅛" seams (see tip on page 84). Press.

7 Trim the block to 12½" square (Figure 6).

ALL TRIANGLES
SHOULD BE
SIMILAR SIZES

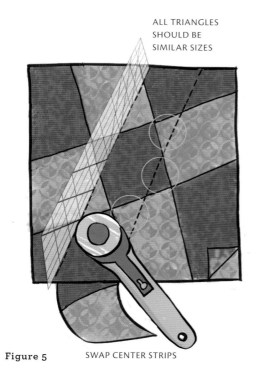

Figure 5   SWAP CENTER STRIPS

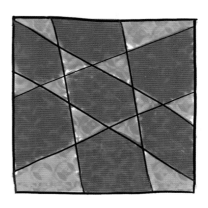

RESEW LAYERS

Figure 6

Make Two Reversible Place Mats

1 Follow steps 1–6 of the block instructions with two contrasting fabric rectangles for each place mat. Change the cutting numbers and angles to those on the place mat diagram (Figure 1):

- First cut: Measure 4" in from top left corner and 4" in from bottom right corner. This strip should be approximately 4½" wide. Swap and sew.

- Second cut: Rotate the fabric 90 degrees to the left. Measure 6" in from the upper left corner and 6" in from the lower right corner. This strip should be approximately 5½" wide. Swap and sew.

- Third cut: Preview the triangles as in block step 5 and Figure 5. Cut a strip approximately 5½" wide from the bottom left side to the top right side. Swap and sew.

Seams So Tiny

Yes, ⅛" seams are correct here. These star points will always have gaps between them (see photo on page 80). Minimize this by sewing narrower final seams. Pin these seams from the center out (and maybe stretch the bias just a bit) to get the points as close as possible. With stars, it's the illusion that counts.

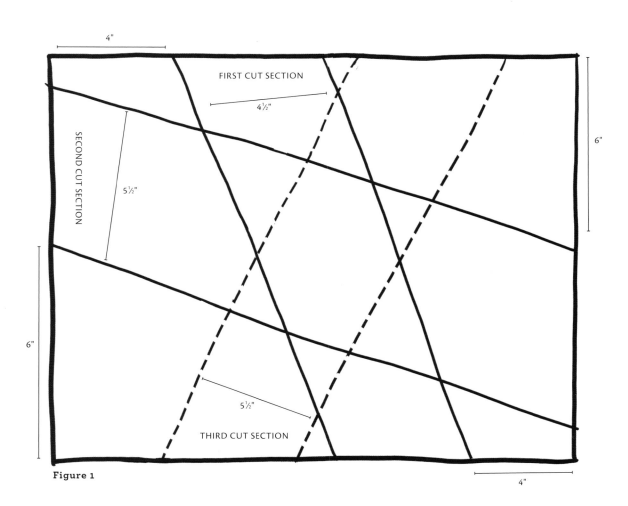

Figure 1

2 Repeat the same cutting and sewing steps to make a second pair of stars.

3 Trim the batting to the same size as the patchwork rectangles. Align the top edges of the two star rectangles right-sides out, with the top edge of the batting in the middle (Figure 2).

4 Baste or safety pin the place mat layers together. Quilt rows at 2" intervals parallel to a diagonal seam.

5 Trim and square the edges to approximately 13" × 16". Bind as explained on page 120–121.

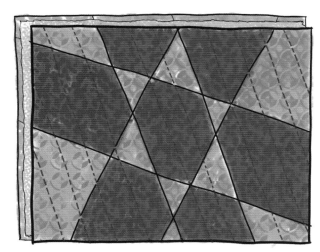

Figure 2

Jaunty Star Mini-Blocks

To make the mini-blocks, follow steps 1–5 using new cutting numbers:

1 Stack two fabrics, both right-side up. Cut an 8½" square from both fabrics at once. Mark 2" in from the upper left corner and 2" in from the lower right corner. Cut a 3"-wide strip between these marks.

2 Switch the top and bottom center stripes. Sew each layer together. Press the seams toward the darker fabric.

3 Restack the two pieces right-side up with the seams aligned. Rotate the stack 90 degrees to the left. Repeat steps 1–2, this time marking 1½" in from the bottom left and top right corners. Cut a 3"-wide strip between these marks.

4 Switch the top and bottom center stripes. Using ¼" seam allowance, sew each layer together. Press the seams toward the darker fabric. Match the seams as best you can.

5 Restack the two pieces right-side up with the seams aligned. Cut a center strip approximately 2¼" wide through both pieces together. Before cutting, stand the ruler on edge to preview the cut. Check to see that the small triangles formed on both sides of each cut will all be about equal sizes. This is more important than whether the cuts are parallel.

6 Swap the middle sections and sew the layers together as before, using only ⅛" seams. Press.

7 Trim the block to 6½" square.

CHAPTER 4

Combination Blocks

I designed each of the blocks in this chapter by combining techniques from designs used earlier in the book. The introduction for each block tells which blocks inspired it. If you're a new quilter, it's a good idea to try the basic blocks first. If you're an experienced quilter, forge ahead!

Now that you know the design secret, try combining techniques yourself to create a totally new block. I'd love to see photos of the new blocks you create—email them to me at Joy@Joy-Lily.com.

TUSCAN SUN BLOCK

Heat Wave Quilt

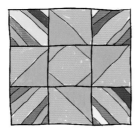

This block combines elements of three different blocks seen earlier in the book. The sun rays are the same units as in the cocktail glasses in the Tipsy-Turvy block (page 40), the center is a Snow Flower petal (page 30) and the corners are Lattice Alone mini-blocks (page 54). If this block looks complicated, you are in for a pleasant surprise, especially if you have already made the three base blocks.

Finished quilt: 60" × 73"

Materials, Tools and Cutting Instructions

FOR ONE BLOCK:

* **¼ yard of background fabric**
  * Cut five 4⅝" squares (background).

* **¼ yard of sun fabric**
  * Cut one 3½" square. Cut the square twice on the diagonal for a total of four triangles (center).
  * Cut two 4⅝" squares. Cut each once on the diagonal for a total of four triangles (rays).
  * Cut four 2" × 8" strips (lattices).

* **¼ yard muslin** (base fabric)
  * Cut four 4¾" squares

* **Assorted fabric strips in coordinating colors** (lattice corners)
  * Cut assorted strips in varied widths from 1½"–2½". Cut up the longer strips only as needed.

TOOLS:

* Basic cutting and sewing tools

FOR THE QUILT:

* **2 yards of orange fabric** (sun background, rays, centers)
  * Cut seven 4⅝" × 42"/44" strips. From these strips, cut fifty 4⅝" squares (rust sun background).
  * Cut three 4⅝" × 42"/44" strips. From these strips, cut twenty 4⅝" squares. Cut each square diagonally into two triangles (rays).
  * Cut one 3½" strip. From it, cut ten 3½" squares (centers).

* **1 yard of yellow fabric** (sun background, centers)
  * Cut seven 4⅝" × 42"/44" strips. From these strips, cut fifty 4⅝" squares (sun background).

* **2¼ yards of rust fabric** (rays, outer border, binding)
  * Cutting parallel to the selvage, cut four 4¾" strips the entire length (outer border).
  * Cutting parallel to the selvage, cut three 2¼" × 81" strips (binding).
  * Cut twenty 4⅝" squares. Cut these squares diagonally into two triangles (rays).

* **¼–½ yard each of six to eight coordinating fabrics, plus remaining rust, red, orange and yellow fabrics.** Use scraps of other fabrics too, if you like (lattice strips).
  * From each fabric, cut one strip in each of the following widths: 1½", 1¾" and 2". (You may need to cut more strips later.)

* **1½ yards of muslin fabric** (base fabric for lattices)
  * Cut ten 4¾" × 42"/44" strips. From these strips, cut eighty 4¾" squares.

* **¾ yard of red fabric** (inner border)
  * Cutting parallel to the selvage, cut twelve 1½" × 27" strips.

* 64" × 77" of thin batting

* Thread to match binding color

TOOLS:

* Basic cutting and sewing tools

Make the Tuscan Sun Block

1 Sew one sun center square (Figure 1): Place the four small triangles right-side down in the center of a right-side up background square; the 90-degree corners of the triangles should point to the center of the square. Position each triangle so both tips hang ¼" over the edge of the square (Figure 2). Sew a ¼" seam across the longest side of each triangle. Flip the triangles right-side up and press. If needed, trim the edges of the triangles even with the background square.

2 Sew four sun ray squares (Figure 3): Place one large triangle right sides together with a square of background fabric. Position the triangle so both tips hang ¼" over the edge of the square (Figure 2). Sew a ¼" seam across the longest side of the triangle. Flip the triangle right-side up and press. If needed, trim the edges of the triangle even with the background square (Figure 4). Repeat to make three additional sun ray squares. The completed squares need not be exactly alike.

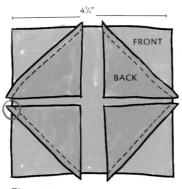

4¾"

FRONT

BACK

Figure 1

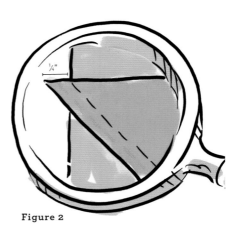

¼"

Figure 2

The Fudge Factor

If the flipped triangle falls a bit short of covering the square, but it's within ¼" of the edge, there's no need to rip and redo it. The triangle edges will be caught in an adjoining seam later.

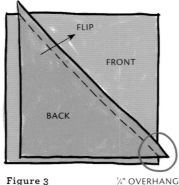

FLIP

FRONT

BACK

Figure 3

¼" OVERHANG

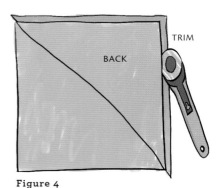

TRIM

BACK

Figure 4

Tuscan Sun Mini-Block

Begin with 2⅝" squares instead of 4⅝" squares. Follow steps 1 – 4 for the center block. Make the lattice strips in steps 3 only 1½" wide. Make the stripes even thinner. Make the snowball triangles from scraps.

3 Sew four lattice squares: Place a 2" strip of background fabric right-side up diagonally across a muslin square. Lay a different color strip right-side down on top of the first strip. Line the strips up at one edge. Sew ¼" seam along that edge to simultaneously sew the strips together and to the muslin square. Flip open the top strip and finger press (Figure 5). Sew and press consecutive strips from the center strip outward on both sides until fabric strips cover the entire base square (Figure 6). Mix up colors and widths of strips (Figure 7). Press, then turn the square to the back and trim the overhanging strips and square to 4⅝" (Figure 8). Repeat to make three additional lattice squares.

4 Position the nine trimmed squares as shown in the diagram (Figure 9). Sew the blocks together in three rows, and then sew the rows together. Press the seams open. Trim the block to 12½" square.

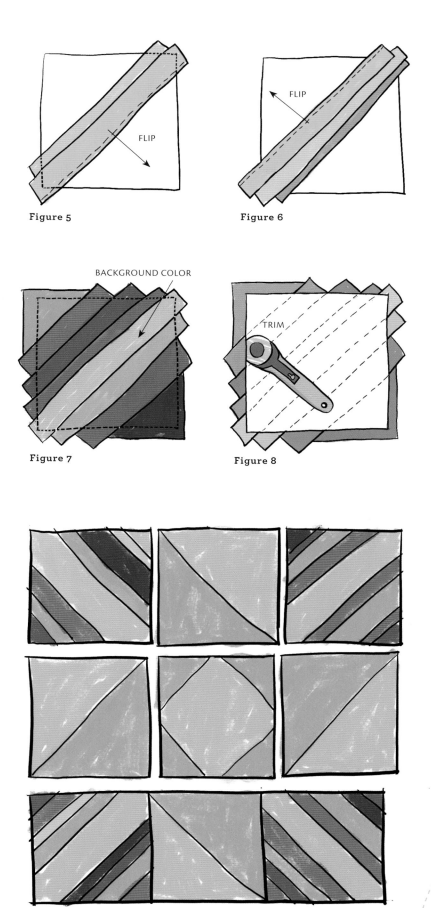

Figure 5

Figure 6

BACKGROUND COLOR

Figure 7

TRIM

Figure 8

Figure 9

Make the Heat Wave Quilt

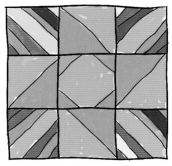

1 Make twenty blocks, ten with an orange background and ten with a yellow background, as in steps 1–4 of the block instructions:

For the yellow background blocks: Make ten sun center squares using the yellow squares and the small orange triangles. Make forty sun ray squares using the yellow squares and the large orange triangles. Make forty lattice squares using a 4¾" muslin square with a yellow strip in the middle. Trim and sew together as described in the block instructions. Press and trim to 12½" square to make ten yellow background blocks (Figure 1).

For the orange background blocks: Make ten sun center squares using the orange squares and the small rust triangles. Make forty sun ray squares using the orange squares and the large rust triangles. Make forty lattice squares using a 4¾" muslin square with an orange strip in the middle. Trim and sew together as described in the block instructions. Press and trim to 12½" square to make ten orange background blocks (Figure 2).

Figure 1

Figure 2

Change Colors to Make a Different Quilt

This quilt design has great possibilities in different color schemes.

- Try a monochromatic version in blue and white or your favorite color combination (pages 20–21).

- Make it in blues, greens, teals and seafoam (bright white) for an undersea look with starfish.

- Make each star a different flower color and everything else in shades of leaf greens for a delightful garden quilt.

- Use blues, purples and black with silver accents for a starry night sky.

- Make it completely scrappy with all your leftovers, for the memories of other quilts.

Remember to use contrasting values for the stars and the backgrounds.

Quilt by Laurel Bross. Photo by Daniel Bross.

2 Arrange the blocks in five rows of four blocks each, alternating yellow and orange backgrounds.

3 Sew four blocks together for each row. Then sew the rows together. If the corners of the blocks match, that's nice, but it's not critical—the stripes on the corner squares are designed so they don't need to match up. Press. Trim the edges of the quilt even.

4 Sew 1½"-wide red inner border strips together into four long strips. Backstitch and press seams open.

5 Measure the length of the quilt. Cut two rust strips ½" longer than this measurement. Sew a long red strip to one side of each rust border strip. Cut off the excess red strip even with the ends of the side rust borders. (See page 23 for tips to help avoid stretching borders while sewing.)

6 Sew the side borders to the quilt, red edges toward the center. Trim the top and bottom edges flush with the quilt. Sew on the top and bottom borders, red edges toward the center (Figure 3).

7 Trim the quilt edges straight and square. Layer, quilt and bind as explained on pages 116–121.

Figure 3

Snake in the Grass Cushion Cover

This block combines the elements of the Curvy Nine Patch block (page 76) with the Wild Geese block (page 48). After making those two blocks, this one will slither right through your sewing machine.

Materials, Tools and Cutting Instructions

FOR ONE BLOCK:

✳ **One fat quarter or ½ yard of background fabric**

- Cut a 14" square.

- Cut a 6½" x 17" rectangle.

✳ **¼ yard of contrasting fabric** (geese corners)

- Cutting instructions for this fabric are found on page 96, step 3.

TOOLS:

✳ Basic cutting and sewing tools

✳ Optional: file folder for template, pencil, paper scissors, flannel board (see page 24)

FOR THE CUSHION COVERS:

✳ **¾ yard of background fabric** (geese, background, cushion back)

- Cut a 14" square.

- Cut a 6½ " × 17" rectangle (geese centers).

- Cut two 12½ " × 9" rectangles (cushion back).

✳ **¼ yard of contrasting fabric** (geese corners)

- See the block instructions for the cutting instructions.

✳ **3 ounces of coordinating yarn (tassels)**

✳ Bobbin thread and top thread to match background color

✳ 14" pillow form

TOOLS:

✳ Basic cutting and sewing tools

✳ Large-eyed sharp needle

✳ Needle threader for yarn

✳ Optional: file folder for template, pencil, paper scissors, flannel board (see page 24)

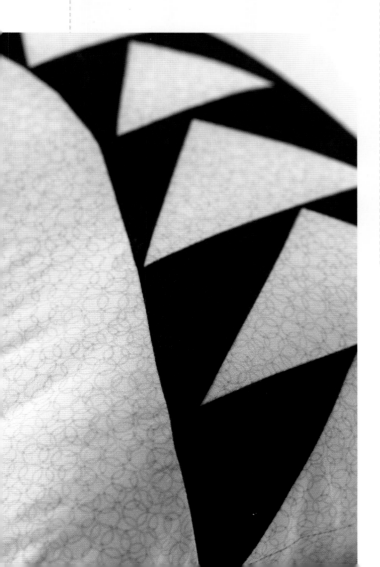

Make The Roman Snake Block

1 From the 6½" × 17" rectangle, cut a gently curved long wedge (Figure 1). The width of the wedge should taper from 6½" at the base to 2" at the top. (You may want to make and follow a template.)

2 Cut the curved wedge into segments in the following sizes, top to bottom: 1⅛", 1¼", 1½", 2", 2¼", 2½", 2¾" and 3½" (Figure 2). Lay the pieces in size order on a flannel board.

3 Cut one contrasting fabric square for each curve segment; this square should be about ½" larger than the height of the segment. (For example, for the 3½" tall segment, cut a 4" contrast fabric square.) Cut each square once on the diagonal into two equal triangles (Figure 2). Lay each pair of triangles together with its related segment.

4 Make the geese units one at a time by sewing the contrasting fabric triangles to their corresponding background segment. With right sides together, sew a triangle to one side of the background segment so that when opened, the triangle completely covers the corner of the rectangle. (See the Flip Tip on page 49). Finger press the seam open (Figure 3).

5 After sewing the first triangle, align and sew the second triangle. The triangles may overlap about ¼" at the center top. The resulting "goose" triangle in the middle of each segment may or may not have a point or be symmetrical. Press.

6 From the back side of the fabrics, trim the overhanging triangle fabric even with the edges of the segment shapes. Repeat steps 4–6 to turn all eight segments into geese.

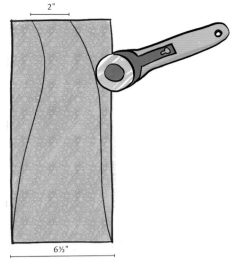

2"

6½"

Figure 1

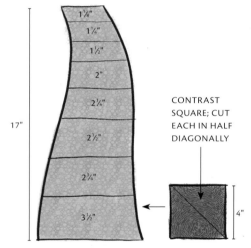

17"

1⅛"
1¼"
1½"
2"
2¼"
2½"
2¾"
3½"

CONTRAST SQUARE; CUT EACH IN HALF DIAGONALLY

4"

Figure 2

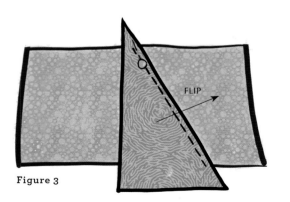

FLIP

Figure 3

7 Using ¼" seam, sew the geese back together in order (Figure 4). Keeping your geese in order on a flannel board as you sew can really help this process. After the wedge is reassembled, it will be only about 14" tall. Don't trim it yet.

8 Center the wedge of geese on top of the 14" square of background fabric, both right-side up. Align the top edges. (If the wedge is a little longer at the bottom, that's okay. If it's too short, resew some seams with slightly smaller seam allowances.)

9 Rotary cut a gently curved line through all layers just inside the edge of the geese wedge on both sides (Figure 5). Use your ruler to hold down the nearby fabric while making the cut. (Use your template here too.) Remove the wedge of background fabric.

10 Starting with the tops of the units aligned, sew the left and right background pieces to the wedge. (See page 77 for a tip on sewing curved seams.) Press the curved seams outward (Figure 6).

11 Trim the block to 12½" square, trimming only the bottom and sides, not the top edge.

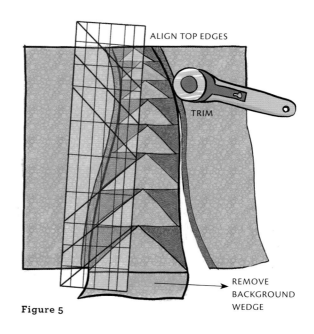

ALIGN TOP EDGES

TRIM

REMOVE BACKGROUND WEDGE

Figure 5

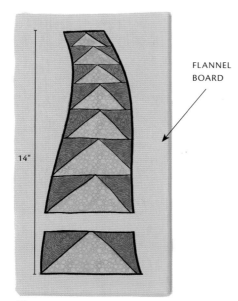

FLANNEL BOARD

14"

Figure 4

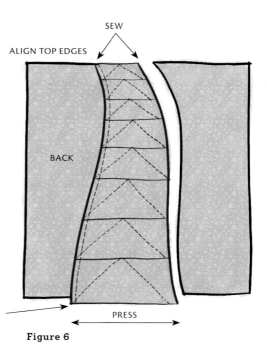

SEW

ALIGN TOP EDGES

BACK

EXTRA AT THE BOTTOM IS ALRIGHT

PRESS

Figure 6

Make the Snake in the Grass Cushion Cover

1 Make one Roman Snake block following steps 1–11 of the block instructions.

2 On both 12½" × 9" background pieces, press ¼" fold toward the back along one 12½" side.

3 On piece A, fold under ¼" again and press the narrow hem. For piece B, fold the edge under 2½"–3" and press this wide hem (Figure 1).

4 With matching thread in the top and bobbin, stitch close to the folded edge of both hems (Figure 1).

5 Lay piece B right sides together with the block. Align the bottom raw edges. The hem is near the center (Figure 2).

6 Lay piece A face down on top of the other pieces, with the raw edge aligned at the top and the hem toward the center (Figure 3). Pin the layers together noticing where the back pieces overlap. Turn the stack over so the block is on top (Figure 4). Pin again all around the edges. Then remove the underside pins.

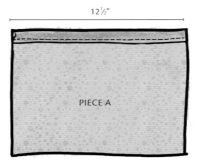

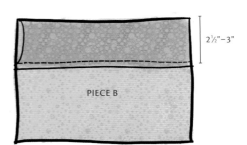

Figure 1

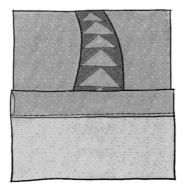

Figure 2

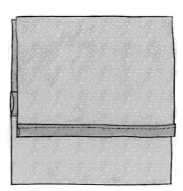

Figure 3

7 Sew a ¼" seam along all four edges. When turning corners, keep the needle in the fabric. Backstitch where the hems overlap to add extra stability. Clip the seam allowance at the corners close to the stitching (Figure 4). Turn the cover right-side out.

8 To add tassels, thread 3 yards of yarn on a needle with a large eye and sharp point. Sew six or more loops of yarn, each about 3" long, through one corner of the pillow cover. With the yarn still attached to the needle, wrap the yarn a few times at the base of the bundle of loops. Knot the yarn at the back. Then slip the needle between the bundle of loops and the binding wraps (Figure 5). Cut the loops open and trim as desired. Repeat to add tassels to the remaining corners of the pillow.

9 A 14" commercial pillow form will fill the cushion cover snugly. (The inside pillow should always be a bit bigger than the cover.) Stuff the form halfway under the narrow-hemmed back flap. Push it into the corners. Force the other half of the back pillow cover over the form (the backstitching will hold the seams where the back pieces join). Sit and bounce on the finished cushion to adjust the filling. If the corners are still empty, stuff them each with a bit of poly-fill or cotton.

CUT LOOPS

SLIP NEEDLE THROUGH BINDING WRAPS

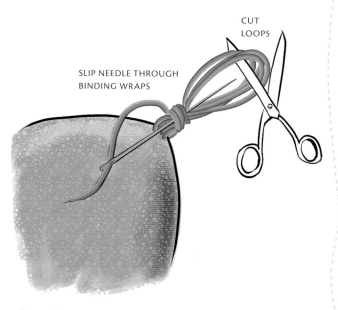

CLIP CORNERS

BACKSTITCH

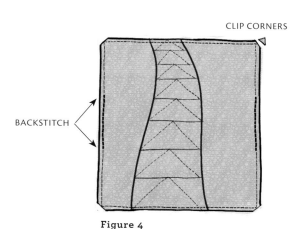

Figure 4

Figure 5

Roman Snake Mini-Block

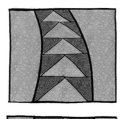
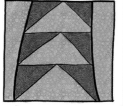

Use either the largest three segments or the smallest five segments of the full-size block. Sew them together as in block step 7. Cut the background fabric 7¾" wide × 7" high. Continue as for the large block. Trim the final mini-block to 6½" square. When trimming the mini-blocks, trim excess fabric from the bottom, preserving the top (smallest) triangles.

Leaf Cover Quilt

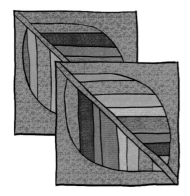

I've been trying for years to piece a realistic-looking leaf block, veins and all. When I finally figured out how to, I got two! The Lazy Leaves block combines the easy curve sewing technique of the Curvy Nine Patch block (page 76) with strata inspired by the Lattice Alone block (page 54). The LEAF COVER QUILT is fun to make because you create a new stripe combination for every two blocks. You can even incorporate scraps leftover from other projects.

Finished quilt: 59" × 80"

Materials, Tools and Cutting Instructions

FOR TWO BLOCKS:

✻ **½ yard background fabric in one or two colors** (background, leaf strata, veins, leaf stripes)

- Cut two 14" squares. Cut both squares in half diagonally, at or near the corners (background).
- Cut four 1" × 18" strips (leaf strata, veins).

✻ **Assorted fabric strips in contrasting colors** (leaf stripes)

- Cut nine to ten 18" long strips in various widths, from 1"–2" wide.

TOOLS:

✻ Basic cutting and sewing tools

✻ 12½" square ruler

✻ File folder

✻ Paper scissors

✻ Pencil

FOR THE QUILT:

✻ **2½ yards of brown fabric** (large and small block backgrounds, borders, binding, veins, appliqué corners). Use leftover fabric for spacers and strata (see below).

- Parallel to the selvage, cut two 7" x 72" strips (borders).
- Parallel to the selvage, cut three 2¼" strips of the entire 2½ yards, plus an extra 30" x 2¼" strip (binding).
- Cut two 14" squares and two 8" squares (large and small backgrounds).
- Cut two 1" x 18" strips and two 1" x 12" strips (veins).
- Cut four 8" squares (appliqué corners).

✻ **2 yards of light gold fabric** (large and small block backgrounds, borders, veins). Use leftover fabric for spacers, strata (see below).

- Parallel to the selvage, cut two 7" x 72" strips (borders).
- Cut two 14" squares and two 8" squares (large and small backgrounds).
- Cut two 1" x 18" strips and two 1" x 12" strips (veins).

✻ **1¼ yard each of six coordinating background colors** (large and small backgrounds, veins)

- Cut two 14" squares and two 8" squares (large and small backgrounds).
- Cut two 1" x 18" strips and two 1" x 12" strips (veins).

✻ From all eight fabric colors, other scraps (main strata, mini-strata)

- From any color cut one more 8" square, and a matching 1" x 12" strip (vein, ninth mini-block). Note there will be one pair of strata triangles leftover.
- Cut a total of seventy strips in varying widths between 1¼"–2" x 18" long (strata).
- Cut about fifty strips in varying widths between 1"–1¾" x 10" long (mini-strata).

✻ Using leftover brown and two more colors, cut two 7" squares and two 7" x 9½" rectangles from each (spacers for mini-blocks).

✻ 63" x 84" of thin batting

✻ Thread to match binding color

TOOLS:

✻ Basic cutting and sewing tools

✻ 12½" square ruler

✻ File folder

✻ Paper scissors

✻ Pencil

Make the Lazy Leaves Blocks

1 Sew together the contrasting color strips, including two of the background color, to make a strata about 9" high and 18" long (Figure 1). Press seams all to one side. Press again from the front to flatten any folds. See the sidebar about creating the look of veins in your leaf.

2 Fold the strata in half width-wise so it forms a square. Make a diagonal cut from the bottom left to the top right. Open the center triangle and cut it in half on the fold line (Figure 2). This creates two different pairs of triangles, A and B.

3 Place a 14" square of background fabric right-side up on the cutting mat. Make a diagonal cut corner to corner. Move one triangle to create a 1" gap between the pieces. Atop these two pieces, place the two A strata triangles. Their diagonal cut edges should meet in the middle of the gap forming a V with a non-matching, carefree look for your leaves (Figure 3). Put a pin through both layers to hold each strata triangle in position.

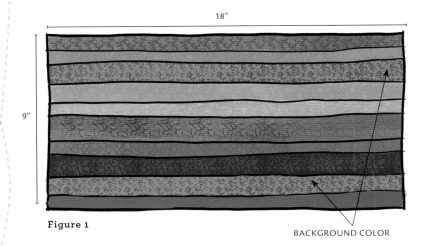

Figure 1

18"

9"

BACKGROUND COLOR

Create Veins

To really create the illusion of veins on the leaf, include two background-color strips of fabric. When piecing the strata in step 1, sew one background strip one row up from the bottom and the other background strip two rows down from the top.

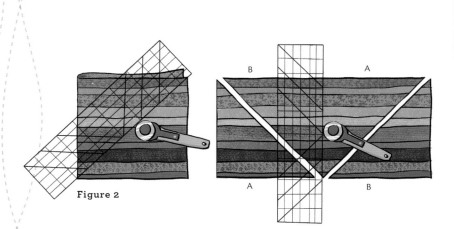

Figure 2

B   A

A   B

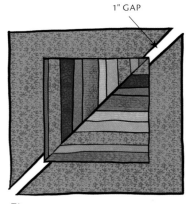

1" GAP

Figure 3

4 To make the leaf pattern, cut a triangle of file folder board the size of a strata triangle using paper scissors. Draw a curve across the square corner to shape a simple half-leaf. Cut the curve as smoothly as possible (Figure 4).

5 Position the leaf pattern on top of the strata, aligning the long edges. Rotary cut around the curve, cutting through the strata and the background all at once. Flip the pattern over and repeat on the other side. Remove the half-leaf shapes of background fabric from under the strata (Figure 5).

6 Find the center of the curved edge of strata and of the background fabric by folding each one in half. Finger press to mark the centers. Place the curved edges of the strata and background right sides together. Line up the centers and pin. With your fingers, match up the two edges, working from the center outward. Handle gently to avoid stretching the bias. Pin at the top (Figure 6). There may be 1/4" of strata hanging beyond the top and bottom, or the strata may be a bit short; either is alright.

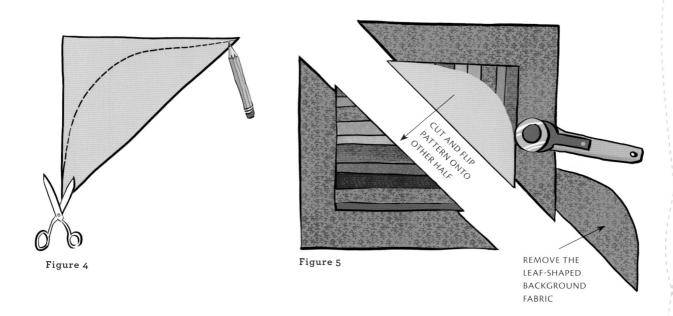

Figure 4

Figure 5

CUT AND FLIP
PATTERN ONTO
OTHER HALF

REMOVE THE
LEAF-SHAPED
BACKGROUND
FABRIC

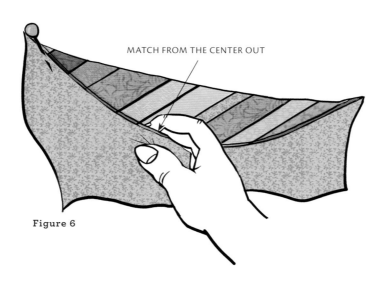

MATCH FROM THE CENTER OUT

Figure 6

7 With the background fabric on top, sew a scant ¼" seam along the curved edge (Figure 7). (See page 77 for tips on sewing curved seams.) Press curve seam outward.

8 Trim the diagonal background edges flush with edges of the strata. Using ¼" seam allowance, sew a 1" × 18" background strip to one diagonal edge (Figure 8). Line up the tips of both halves of the leaf and sew the second half to the center strip. Some leaf tips may be too lazy to line up exactly—never mind! Trim each block to 12½" square.

9 Repeat block steps 5 – 8 for the second block.

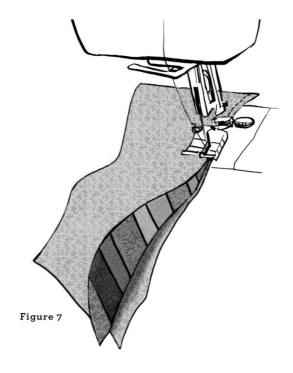

Figure 7

Leaf Variations

Make patterns with deep or shallow curves for different-shaped leaves. Vary the diagonal cut of the background up to 2" off the top left and bottom right corners to tilt some of the leaves a bit differently.

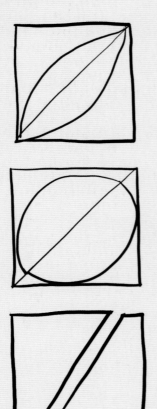

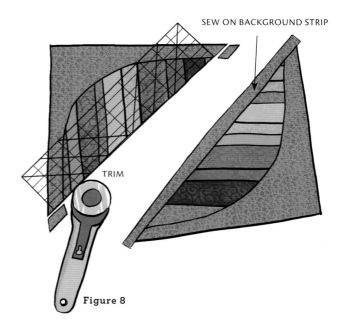

SEW ON BACKGROUND STRIP

TRIM

Figure 8

Make the Leaf Cover Quilt

1 Following the block instructions, make sixteen leaf blocks with the 14" squares of background fabrics. Vary the strata sets among the background fabric colors. Trim to 12½" square.

2 Use the 8" squares to make nine mini-blocks. Using the narrower strips, sew five sets of mini-strata, each measuring 5" × 10". Cut and sew the mini-blocks in the same way you did the large blocks.

3 Arrange the blocks, mini-blocks and spacers as shown in the diagram (Figure 1). Use one spacer color per row. (It may take some juggling to arrange colors so each large leaf is adjacent to contrasting colors.) Sew the blocks together to make four rows of four large blocks each and three rows of mini-blocks and spacers. Sew the rows together. Press the quilt and even up the edges.

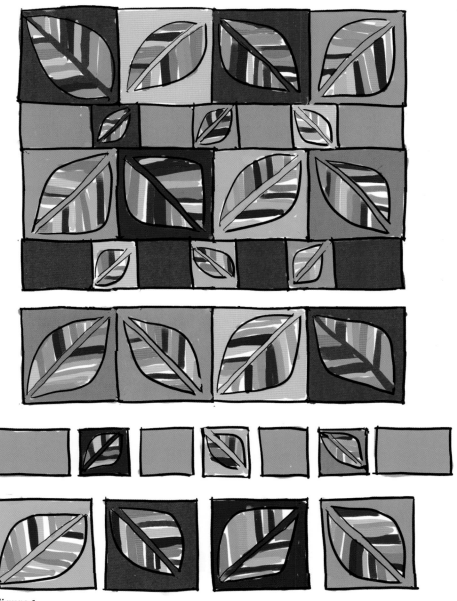

Figure 1

4 To make the border, stack a light gold 7" × 72" fabric strip and a brown 7" × 72" fabric strip, both strips right-side down. On the wrong side of the top fabric, draw a shallow curved pencil line down the middle. Freehand rotary cut along this line (Figure 2). (Practice on some scrap fabric first.) Repeat on the second set of border strips.

5 Swap one half of each border pair (Figure 3). Mark the center of each strip and sew the strips together from the center out. (Use the same technique as sewing the curved leaf blocks together).

Figure 2

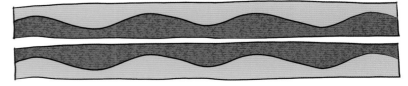

SEW OUT FROM CENTER

Figure 3

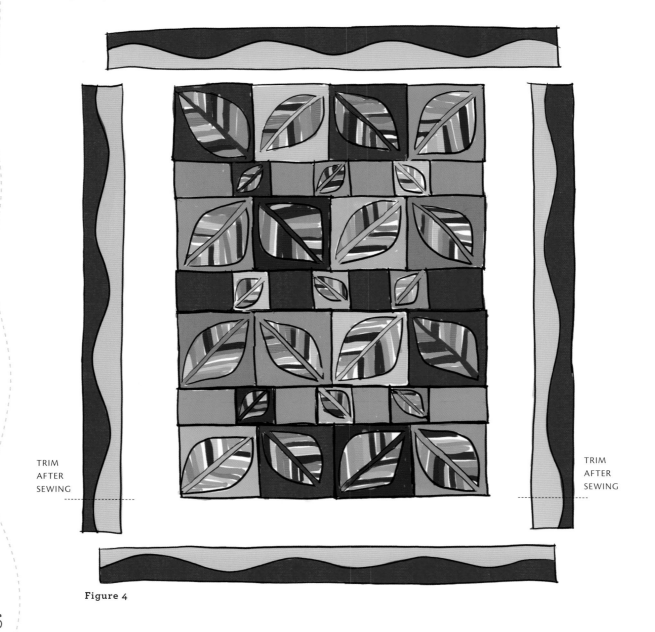

TRIM
AFTER
SEWING

TRIM
AFTER
SEWING

Figure 4

6 Sew a border strip to each side of the quilt with the brown toward the outside. Trim the top and bottom edges even with the quilt. Sew the top and bottom borders to the quilt with the brown on the outside (Figure 4).

7 To round the corners, lay an 8" brown square face up atop one corner. Mark with a pin where the curve touches the edge of the square. Turn the square over and draw a casual quarter circle curve on the back, between the pins. Cut ¼" inside of this curved line. Fold this ¼" over the back of the fabric and press. (The bias will help it curve.) Also press ¼" of two adjacent straight edges to the back (Figure 5). Line up the border curves with the pressed curve; the outside corner edges remain raw. Appliqué the folded curve and adjacent legs of the top piece to the borders with matching thread (Figure 6). Use the invisible binding stitch shown on page 121. Repeat this step for three more curved corners. When quilting, use plenty of stitching across these "cheater corners" to make them blend into the quilt.

8 Layer, quilt and bind as explained on pages 116-121.

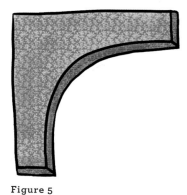

Figure 5

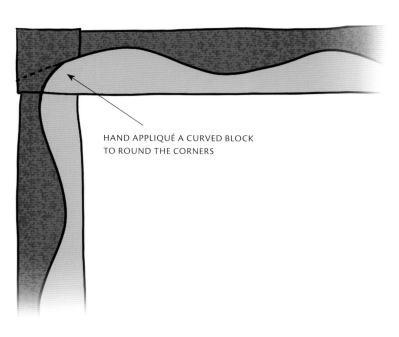

HAND APPLIQUÉ A CURVED BLOCK
TO ROUND THE CORNERS

Figure 6

Carefree Sampler Quilt

When you make each block in this book once (possibly in a coordinated set of colors), you will have a total of nineteen blocks, even though there are only twelve designs. That's because the instructions for each block in Chapter 3 make multiple blocks at the same time. Sew up one more block of your choice (or perhaps a set of four mini-blocks) for a twentieth square. Then you can then assemble a 63" × 81" CAREFREE SAMPLER QUILT—big enough for a double bed. Put it together with sashing strips and cornerstones to frame each block.

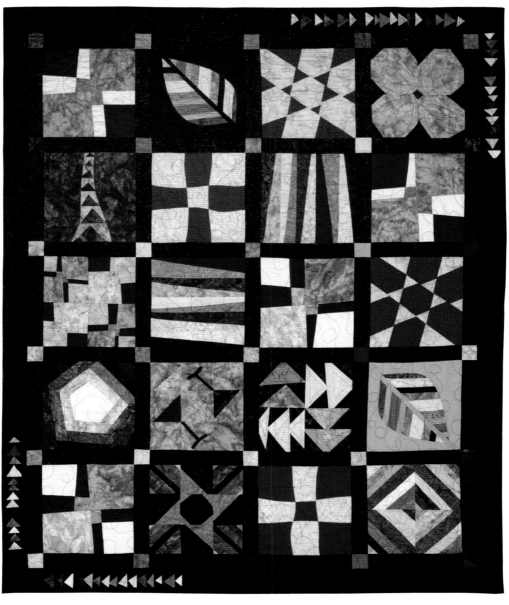

Finished quilt: 63" × 81"

Materials, Tools and Cutting Instructions

FOR THE SAMPLER QUILT:

✳ Twenty 12½" Carefree blocks

✳ **4 yards of very dark fabric** (sashings, borders, border geese triangles, binding)

- Cut off ½ yard and set it aside.

- Cutting parallel to the selvage, cut seven 2½" strips by the whole length of fabric. From four of these strips, cut twenty-nine 13" segments. Leave the rest in long strips (sashings).

- Cutting parallel to the selvage, cut two 4" strips by the whole length of fabric (outer borders). You will sub-cut them in step 13.

- Cutting parallel to the selvage, cut three 2¼" strips the entire length of the fabric (binding).

- Cut eight 1¼" × 24" strips (edges of the border geese).

- From remaining ½ yard of fabric, cut about sixty 2½" squares. Cut each square in half on the diagonal to make triangles (border geese).

✳ **Assorted scraps of fabric from the blocks** (cornerstones, border geese)

- Cut thirty 2½" squares (cornerstones).

- Cut a 2½"-wide strip of each fabric, and sub-cut them for a total of about sixty 1½"–2¼" pieces (border geese).

✳ 67" × 85" of batting

✳ Thread to match binding

TOOLS:

✳ Basic cutting and sewing tools

Make the Carefree Sampler Quilt

1 Make sure that all twenty blocks are trimmed to exactly 12½" square.

2 Using ¼" seams, sew a cornerstone square on the end of the twenty-nine 13" sashing strips (Figure 1). Press the seams open.

3 With right sides together and the blocks on top, chain-sew the edge of the 12½" blocks to the long 2½" sashing strip. Leave ¼" between blocks. (Figure 2).

4 Flip open and press. Cut the blocks apart, trimming the sashing flush with the edges (Figure 3).

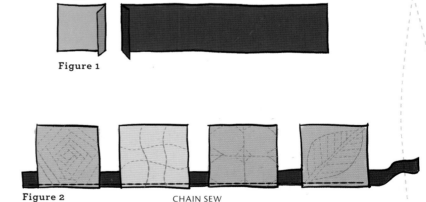

2½"   13"

Figure 1

Figure 2   CHAIN SEW

Figure 3   CUT APART

5 Using ¼" seam, sew a cornerstoned sashing strip (from step 1) to the left edge of each block (Figure 4). Start by matching and pinning the seams at the cornerstone. Finish by trimming the other end of the sashing even with the edge of the block.

6 Lay out all the blocks, cornerstones in the upper left corner, in a pleasing arrangement of five rows, four blocks each. Scatter the strongest colors and the most dramatic shapes around the quilt.

7 Notice that you only need to add additional sashing/cornerstones on the bottom row of blocks and on the right-hand end of each row (Figure 5). Repeat step 5 to add sashing and cornerstones around the blocks at the edges of the quilt. (Be sure to keep the blocks in order.) The very last block on the bottom right will need a little extra help matching the final cornerstone for its bottom right corner. That is the next step.

8 Begin step 5 on the final side of this last block. Stop sewing about 1" before you reach the last cornerstone. Remove the sewing from the machine. Press a fold in the sashing fabric to match the seam above it. Press a ¼" fold on the cornerstone (Figure 6). Match these folds, face to face (see Figure 5, page 79). Then sew the cornerstone onto the adjacent sashing along the folds. Now complete the sashing seam. This last cornerstone will be right where you want it!

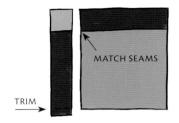

Figure 4

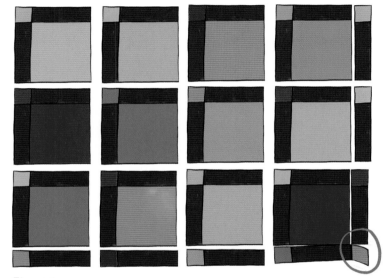

Figure 5

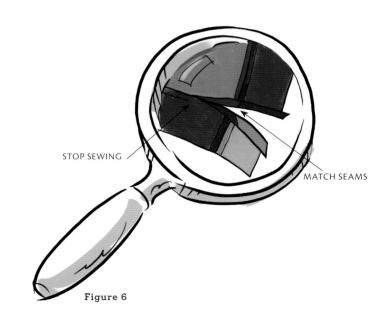

Figure 6

9 Sew the blocks together into rows (Figure 7). Then sew the rows together. Match the seam at each cornerstone. (See page 22 for seam matching hints.)

10 To make the flying geese borders, refer to page 51. For this quilt, though, the rectangle sizes are 2½" wide × assorted heights up to 2¼", and the triangles are made from 2½" squares (listed in the cutting instructions on page 109). After making the individual geese, only trim the long sides of the rectangles.

11 Sew the geese together in four strips of fourteen to eighteen geese each. Keep them all flying the same direction. Trim the long sides of the geese strips.

12 Sew the 1¼" strips of border fabric to both long sides of all four geese strips. Press and trim the top and bottom of all strips as needed.

13 Arrange the geese strips near two opposite corners of the quilt top (Figure 7). Sew a short piece of the 4" wide border strip to one end of each strip of geese and a longer strip to the other end, using the diagram below as a placement guide.

14 Pin and sew the short borders to the top and bottom of the quilt. (Remember to sew with the quilt on top and the strip underneath to avoid getting rippled edges on your quilt.) Press the quilt and trim the ends square.

15 Pin and sew the two long borders to the quilt sides in the same way. Trim the ends square.

16 Layer, quilt and bind as explained on pages 116–121.

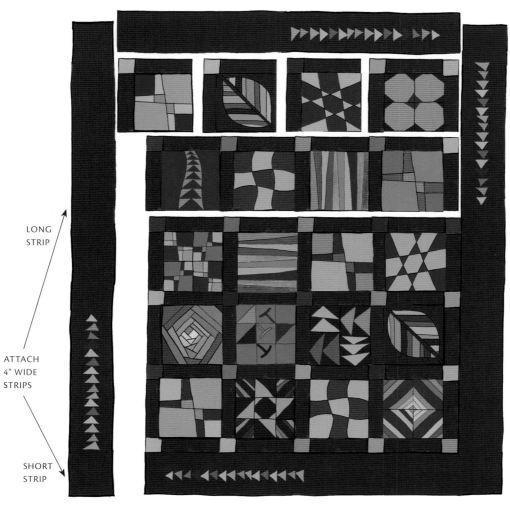

LONG STRIP

ATTACH 4" WIDE STRIPS

SHORT STRIP

Figure 7

Finishing Your Quilt

By definition, a quilt is a sandwich of three layers: the top (which may be made of patchworked fabrics or not), the filling or batting, and the backing fabric. This sandwich needs some stitching to keep those three layers from shifting around and some way to close the edges (usually that's binding).

There are two ways to put the three layers of your quilt together. The typical way is to put the backing face down, lay the batting on it and position the top of the quilt on the batting right-side up. Attach the layers together temporarily with basting safety pins or long basting stitches. Remove them only after the quilting is completed. *Quilting* refers to the stitching that holds the three layers together.

The traditional quilting technique is detailed later in this section, but first, there is a quicker and simpler way to assemble small items like table runners and place mats. The Walk in the Park Table Runner (page 28) and Cocktail Apron (page 40) are put together by the pillowcase method.

This chapter gives you lots of options and ideas for how you can finish your quilt.

Layout Ideas

Chapter 1 explains that you can use any of the twelve blocks for any of the projects in this book. That means you can also use these blocks in almost any quilt layout. Here are four basic arrangements of the 12½" blocks. (Four mini-blocks sewn together will also make a 12½" square.)

A Simple Grid

Sew rows of squares together and then assemble the rows. Refer to page 22 for a technique to make corner matching easy when assembling the rows. The SQUARE DANCE QUILT (page 62), ZIGZAG TOTE BAG (page 52) and WILD GOOSE CHASE WALL QUILT (page 46) are all examples of the grid layout. Often, but not always, the blocks are arranged in contrasting colors to create a checkerboard. The HEAT WAVE QUILT (page 88) and the COCKTAIL APRON (page 40) are checkered this way.

Blocks on Point

When a grid is rotated 45 degrees, corners of the blocks point straight up and down. In the GARDEN PATH QUILT (page 74), the blocks are laid out *on point*. The rows are still assembled in strips, but it's now necessary to add *setting triangles* to square off the edges of the quilt. When cutting these triangles, be careful that the bias-cut edges do not wind up on the outside edge of the quilt. The cutting diagram on page 78 for the setting triangles in the GARDEN PATH QUILT shows how to cut the triangles on the straight of grain.

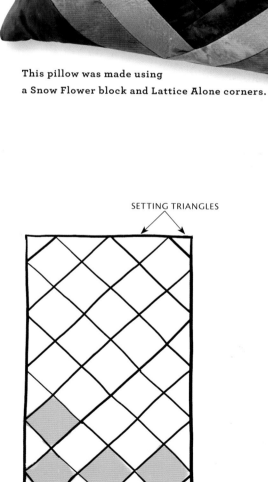

This pillow was made using
a Snow Flower block and Lattice Alone corners.

SETTING TRIANGLES

Simple Grid

Blocks on Point

Bar Quilts

The easiest way to put together a quilt is in bars or large stripes. No seam matching is needed between rows of blocks because there are spacers in between. In the CRAYONS QUILT (page 68), the spacers are black bars. In the LEAF COVER QUILT (page 100), they are rows of mini-leaf blocks.

Sashing to Frame the Blocks

The CAREFREE SAMPLER QUILT (page 108) has strips of a single color that visually set off each block and highlight each design. It also has small squares in the corners between blocks. These "cornerstones" look tricky, but they are actually quite easy to insert with the sashing assembly technique described on pages 109-110. Sashing can also be added in the same way to blocks arranged on the point.

More Quilt Layouts

Flip through quilt magazines to look for the quilt layouts discussed here and others you may want to try. There are many other quilt arrangements not used in this book. Two common ones are the brick pattern and large center medallions surrounded by many borders. You will also see lots of other ideas for using blocks, rectangles, triangles, diamonds and more.

Bar Quilt

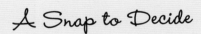

A Snap to Decide

Take a digital photo of different arrangements of your blocks. Compare the photos to decide which design you like best.

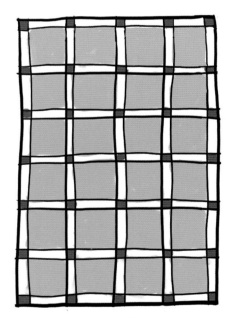

Sashing to Frame the Blocks

Pillowcase Assembly Technique

With this technique, you won't need to bind the finished quilt. The edges are finished when you turn the work right-side out. The pillowcase technique works well on irregular shapes, too. Do not use polyester batting because some pressing will be needed (polyester melts when pressed). If your quilt is larger than about 48" square, I recommend using the standard technique instead (page 116) because a large project will be awkward to assemble by the pillowcase technique.

1 Place the pre-trimmed top and slightly-larger backing right sides together. Place them both on top of the batting with the backside of the quilt top up (Figure 1).

2 Sew the layers together around all sides, ¼" inside the edge of the quilt top. Leave an opening in the middle of one side for turning the work right-side out (Figure 1). The opening should be about one third the length of the side.

3 Clip the corners close to the stitching (Figure 2). Pull the work through the opening. Push out the corners fully and flatten the seams to their full size. Press the seams flat. Press under the raw edges of the opening even with the sides of the project.

4 Slipstitch the opening closed.

5 Stitch around the edge of the project to hold the edges in place (Figure 3). Baste and quilt as desired.

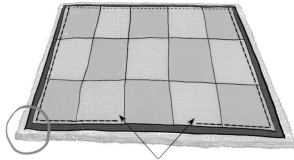

TOP FACE DOWN, BACK FACE UP, BATTING ON THE BOTTOM

LEAVE AN OPENING

Figure 1

Figure 2

TURN RIGHT-SIDE OUT,
TOPSTITCH NEAR THE EDGES AND QUILT

Figure 3

Standard Assembly Technique

To finish a quilt project in the traditional way, you will need a few supplies:

- Quilters' safety pins or quilting straight pins, a long thin needle and thread for basting
- Painters blue masking tape
- Disappearing pen or pencil
- Quilters' ruler

1 Cut or piece the backing and the batting to be at least 2" larger on all sides than the front of the quilt. (Backings always shrink a bit when quilted.)

2 Before you begin to assemble the quilt sandwich, give some thought to what the quilting stitch pattern will be. This is a good time to mark a design on the quilt. Use a disappearing pen or pencil to draw the quilting design on the quilt top.

3 On the biggest table you have available, lay out and tape the backing, right-side down, so it won't move or wrinkle while adding the other layers. Then smooth the batting on top of the backing. (See page 17 for information on different types of batting.) Slide your flat quilting ruler across the batting to help smooth it. If the batting is bigger than the back, trim it to match the size of the backing fabric.

4 Lay the front of the quilt on top of the batting, right-side up. Smooth it out. Leave equal amounts of batting and backing showing on all four sides. (Don't tape down the batting or top.)

5 Pin a row across the middle of the quilt through all three layers. Be sure to include any borders. From that anchor row, pin rows down to the bottom and up to the top of the quilt at 2"–3" intervals. Try not to lift the sandwich up from the table while pinning. You may need to smooth the quilt with your hand as you pin, but never smooth it on the diagonal, because doing so may stretch the fabric.

6 When the sandwich is completely pinned, remove the tape from the back. If you used straight pins to pin the layers together, hand sew 3"–4" long stitches through all layers (called *basting*). Baste rows every 3"–4" for hand stitching; baste much closer for machine stitching. There's no need to baste crosswise. If you pinned the layers together using quilters' safety pins, they are the basting and you are ready to quilt. Basting stitches remain in until all the quilting is done. Remove safety pins as they get close to the needle.

Table Strategy

A single table at least as long as the width of your quilt can be used to baste a large quilt. Position the middle of the quilt assembly across the table. Pin only on the part that is flat atop the table. Then lift the tape and slide the whole sandwich backward and forward to reach the overhanging sections.

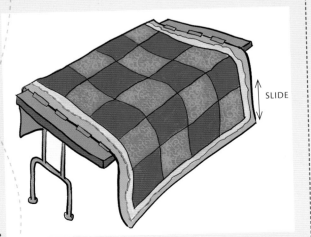

SLIDE

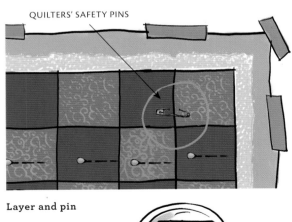

QUILTERS' SAFETY PINS

Layer and pin

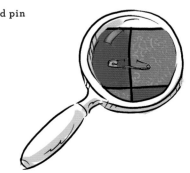

Quilting Your Quilt

There are three different choices for how to permanently hold the quilt sandwich together: tying, hand quilting or machine quilting.

Tying

The simplest and fastest way to secure a quilt sandwich is to tie it. When tying, you can also use heavier batting to make a comforter instead of a thin quilt. To tie a quilt project, you will need a few supplies:

- Long needle with a sharp point and large eye

- Yarn or pearl cotton

- Scissors

- Yarn needle threader

- Optional: thimble

1 Double your yarn or thread and thread your needle. Knot the ends together. (Now you have four strands of thread.)

2 To make a single tie, take a stitch down through all three quilt layers, and back up in almost the same place.

3 Knot the ends securely with 1½ square knots. Place the knots all on the front, or all on the back. Trim the thread or yarn tails to an inch or less. It's faster to sew a whole row of stitches at once, leaving the thread stretched between them. Clip the thread in the middle between the stitches and then tie all the knots in the row. Then trim the knots equally short.

TRIM THREAD BETWEEN TIES

TIE AND CLIP ENDS

Quilting designs and Sashiko patterns

Hand Quilting

Hand quilting is achieved by sewing a running stitch through all three layers. The Amish are famous for making tiny stitches in elegant patterns. The Gee's Bend quilters use gigantic stitches, and they are famous too. Try to make your stitches a uniform size, but don't make them too small to enjoy the process—perhaps more Gee's Bend than Amish. To hand quilt your project, you will need:

- Very short (1½" long) sharp needles

- Hand quilting thread

- Small scissors

- Thimble(s) (a second thimble goes under the fabric)

Many traditional patterns are available in books and as stencils for hand quilting, or you can create your own designs. You can also send your quilt to some enterprising person to hand quilt for you. (Look for advertisements in the back of quilt magazines.)

The Japanese decorate fabric with large contrasting-colored hand stitches sewn with thick thread (think all six strands of embroidery floss). They call this *Sashiko*, and a rich tradition of Sashiko patterns are available. In large scale, Sashiko designs make elegant quilting patterns, too. (See Resources on page 124 for a Sashiko design resource.)

After the quilting is completed, trim the excess batting and square the edges. See the tip on page 73 for hints on squaring edges. Now you're ready for binding.

Hide the Knots

When hand quilting, you can make the beginning and end of each length of thread disappear inside the quilt. Make a loop at the tail end of a length of thread (18" maximum). Pass the needle twice through this loop and pull tight to make a tiny knot. Begin sewing by making the next stitch wherever you need it, down only into the batting and back up. Then gently tug until the knot pops through the layer of fabric. It's gone forever. When you're down to the last 3" of thread, make a similar knot below the needle eye. Take the next stitch into the batting. Stitch back up through the top layer and tug the knot to bury it inside the quilt. Pull slightly on the thread and clip it off right at the fabric.

Machine Quilting

If hand quilting isn't appealing, you can machine quilt your projects on your home sewing machine. A good book for learning machine quilting, including the free-motion technique, is *Quilt as Desired* by Charlene Frable.

Before you begin, practice quilting a small sandwich of the same fabrics and batting as your quilt. Check the stitch size, thread tension and your needle. (Try loosening the top thread tension to get a better stitch.) Use regular sewing machine thread or special quilting thread. I recommend using a walking foot on your machine, unless you are doing free-motion stitching.

Start by rolling up the quilt sandwich so only enough of it is showing to stitch the first row or two. As you complete rows, gradually unroll the work. Always start sewing at the same edge. (Reversing direction on the next row will cause the top fabric to torque between the rows.)

For bigger quilts, I enthusiastically recommend sending them out to someone with a longarm quilting machine. (There are many enterprising individuals who own these large machines and provide quilting services. Look for advertisements in the back of quilt magazines.)

BICYCLE CUFF CLAMP

Quilt, unrolling as you work.

Or you can learn to operate a longarm quilting machine and then rent time on one. I took lessons on a longarm at my local quilt shop, and I quilted most of the large quilts in this book on a longarm machine. The best part of longarm quilting is that you don't need to assemble or baste the quilt sandwich. The machine feeds the three layers together as you work. (Operating a longarm machine is a bit like walking back and forth gripping a pair of vibrating motorcycle handlebars while you draw or follow a pattern with those handlebars. I like to draw freehand, and after the first few quilts, I've gotten comfortable using the longarm machine.)

Once the quilting is completed, trim the excess batting and square the edges. (See the tip on page 73 for hints on squaring edges.) Now you're ready for binding.

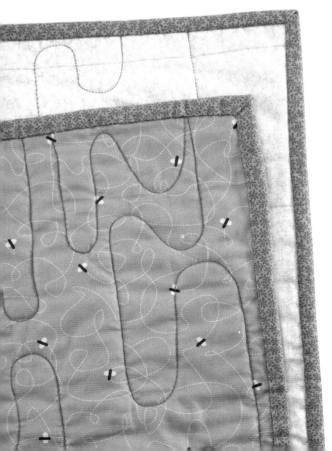

Longarm quilting detail design

Binding Your Quilt

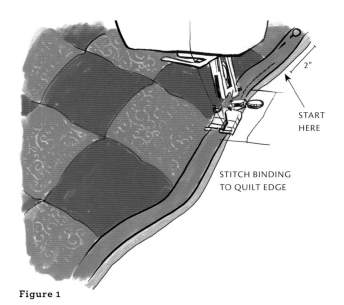

1 Measure the perimeter of your quilt top (two lengths plus two widths). Add 4" more to this total for seams and overlap at the end. This is the total length of binding you'll need to go all the way around your quilt. Quilt fabric is about 40" wide after shrinkage, so divide your total inches by 40. Round up any fractions. This number is how many strips you need when cutting from selvage to selvage. All bindings in this book are cut at 2¼", so to find out how much yardage you need, multiply the number of strips you need by 2¼".

2 Cut the number of 2¼" strips you need. Sew them together end to end, backstitching at the seam edges. Press the seams open, and then fold and press this long strip in half lengthwise, right-side out.

3 Press a ½" fold inside one end of the folded binding. Position this end on the right side of one edge of the quilt, but not at a corner. Align the raw edges of the binding and the raw edge of the quilt. Use one pin to hold the end of the binding strip in place, but start sewing about 2" farther down the binding (Figure 1). Do not pin the rest of the binding in place around the quilt because it will tend to stretch a little as you sew.

4 Sew the binding to the edge of the quilt, staying ¼" from the raw edge until you approach a corner. Stop and mark exactly ¼" from the corner. Resume sewing, but stop exactly at the ¼" mark (Figure 2).

5 Remove the quilt from under the presser foot. Fold the binding upward, away from the quilt corner. Fold a 45-degree angle with its tip at the very corner of the quilt (Figure 2). Then fold the binding strip back toward the quilt and align its cut edge with the next edge of the quilt (Figure 3).

Figure 1

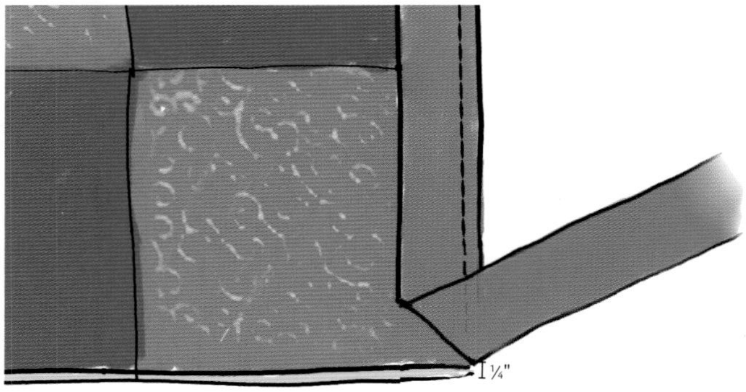

START HERE

STITCH BINDING TO QUILT EDGE

2"

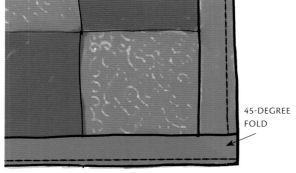

Figure 2

STOP SEWING, FOLD BINDING BACK AT 45-DEGREE ANGLE

1¼"

Figure 3

45-DEGREE FOLD

FOLD BINDING EVEN WITH EDGE

Binders' Math

- inches of quilt top edge (x2) + side (x2) + 4"= perimeter in inches
- (perimeter) divided by 40" (width of fabric) , rounded up to the nearest whole number = XX (number of strips to cut)
- (number of strips to cut) x 2¼" (width of a strip) = inches of yardage needed

6 Start sewing the new side right from the edge. Continue until you approach the next corner. Repeat steps 4–5 to turn three more corners.

7 When you are almost back to the beginning, pause the sewing to overlap the binding. Cut the end of the binding strip just before the point where you began sewing. Keep the small fold at the beginning of the binding in place, but open the long fold. Tuck the cut end of the binding strip inside it (Figure 4). Give a slight tug to make sure the ends are snug. Pin in place and continue sewing straight across the joined ends until you reach the starting point.

8 Fold the binding over the edge of the quilt to the back. It will just cover the stitching line. Fold the back corners into mitered points. Pin down a small section of binding at a time, and hand-stitch the folded edge to the back of the quilt using matching thread and an invisible stitch.

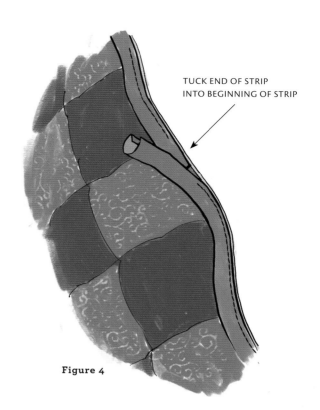

TUCK END OF STRIP
INTO BEGINNING OF STRIP

Figure 4

Invisible Binding Stitch

After hiding the knot (page 118), make the first stitch come up precisely into the fold of the binding. Stitch back into the quilt directly below this spot to form a completely invisible stitch. Travel to the next stitch location through the batting. Don't stitch through to the quilt top. Repeat, repeat, repeat . . .

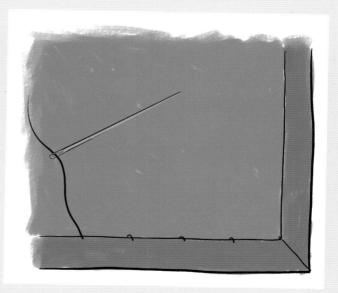

Endless Possibilities

No matter what colors you like or quilt size you need, there's a way to make your own unique quilt based on the projects and block patterns in this book. I've made lots of variations using these blocks. Shown below and throughout the book are several examples of ways to mix and match blocks and change the colors to make quilts that look altogether new. Enjoy!

COLOR VARIATION OF THE *SQUARE DANCE QUILT* (PAGE 67)

STRATA INSTEAD OF SOLID FABRIC IN THE *GEE WHIZ WEDGE* BLOCK (PAGE 68)

APPLIQUÉ EMBELLISHED CORNERS

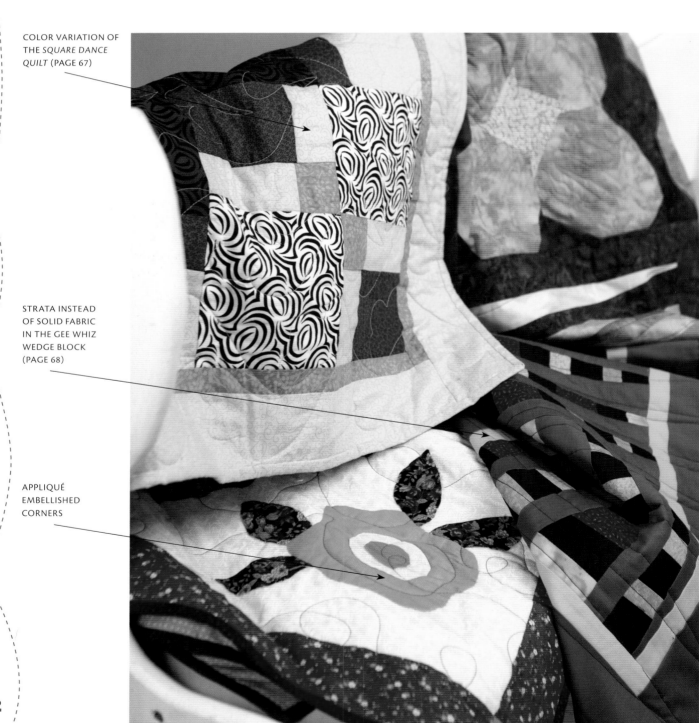

Photo by Alfred Castino

About the Author

Joy-Lily's sewing genes go back to the dawn of history. An early ancestor invented the needle—really! Her mother and grandfather sewed clothes for a living. Parting with family tradition, she trained to be a graphic artist at Cass Tech and College of Art & Design in Detroit. She freelanced in New York as an illustrator and print designer before the dawn of computer graphics.

She returned to the textile fold on the streets of Manhattan: selling underwear batik-dyed in her own designs began to overtake her graphics work. Joy-Lily's textile art repertoire has since expanded to screen printing, marbling fabric, stamp art, natural dyeing, shibori, silk painting, fabric collage, felting and art quilting. Her art cloth has also been turned into commercial quilt fabric. Plain fabric is just not safe around her!

A California Arts Council grant allowed her to teach classes in quilting, silk painting and fabric printing at a San Francisco senior center for eleven years. Currently she teaches a wide range of fabric art techniques (including free-style quilting) to textile guilds, adult education classes and at art centers.

Joy-Lily's quilt designs have appeared in major quilt magazines. Her art quilts have been published and exhibited internationally. She continues to play where the fabric-edge meets art. This is her first book. See more of her art at www.joy-lily.com .

Resources

Fabrics and Threads

AMY BUTLER DESIGNS
www.amybutlerdesign.com

COATS AND CLARK
www.coatsandclark.com
(threads and chart of thread uses)

HOFFMAN FABRICS
www.hoffmanfabrics.com

P & B TEXTILES
www.pbtex.com

Batting

FAIRFIELD
www.fairfieldworld.com

QUILTERS DREAM BATTING
www.quiltersdreambatting.com
(Dream Green batting made from
recycled bottles)

THE WARM COMPANY
www.warmcompany.com
(Warm & Natural and Warm &
White batting)

Fusibles and Interfacings

MISTYFUSE
www.mistyfuse.com

PELLON
www.pellonideas.com
(Wonder Under, Peltex stabilizer
for totes, fusible interfacing)

Tools

FISKARS
www2.fiskars.com/Products/
Sewing-and-Quilting/Sewing-
and-Quilting-Tools
(rotary cutters, rulers, cutting
mats, scissors)

MARTELLI
www.martellinotions.com
(ergonomic rotary cutters)

OLFA
www.olfa.com
(rotary cutters, rulers,
cutting mats)

Red & green value viewing cards
www.createforless.com/Cottage
+Mills+Color+Evaluator+II+Red/
Green+Filter/pid9842.aspx

Books

*Cut Loose Quilts: Stack,
Slice, Stitch, and Sew*
by Jan Mullen

*Digital Painting Fundamentals
with Corel Painter 12*
by Rhoda Grossman
(aka Rhoda Draws)

Liberated Quiltmaking II
by Gwen Marston

Quilt As Desired
by Charlene Frable

*That Dorky Homemade Look:
Quilting Lessons from a
Parallel Universe*
by Lisa Boyer

The Magical Effects of Color
by Joen Wolfrom

*The Quilts of Gee's Bend:
Masterpieces from a Lost Place*
by William Arnett

*The Ultimate Sashiko Sourcebook:
Patterns, Projects and Inspirations*
by Susan Briscoe

Magazines

McCalls Quilting
www.mccallsquilting.com

Quilters Home
www.quiltershomemag.com

Quilters Newsletter Magazine
www.quiltersnewsletter.com

Events

www.americanquilter.com
(Four major quilt shows in central
U.S. each year)

www.quiltguilds.com
(Locate quilt guilds in your area.)

www.quiltfest.com
(Seven major quilt shows in the
U.S. each year.)

www.quilts.com/newHome/con-
tests/index.php
(Five major quilt shows in the U.S.
each year.)

Index

*This book is dedicated
to the muse of carefree quilters.
Her name is Catawampus.*

Acknowledgements

It takes a village to write a quilt book, I've discovered. Many of my students sewed early versions of these blocks, helping to untangle the instructions. Blocks for the HEAT WAVE QUILT were assembled by Karen Biewer, Julie Ferrari, Julie Hirsch, Joan Kelleher, Maureen Lennon, Judy McPhee and Terry Mullen from my Quilting Connection class at San Mateo Adult School.

My assistant Judy George is a whiz on the computer as well as on the sewing machine. She sew-tested all the block instructions, making the sampler quilt in the process. She also formatted, proof-read and attempted to keep me organized. And with her other hand she made lunch.

Rhoda Draws has raised the bar on DIY illustrations. Her fresh, casual drawing style adds pizzazz to the book.

The Ladies of the Longarm, with their machines and expertise, made finishing the quilts smooth sailing: Kit, Roberta, Tamara, Geri and Evelyn at Always Quilting, Linda Hannawalt at San Francisco Sewing & Quilting Collaborative and June Broughton in Redding, CA. May your bobbins always finish at the end of the row.

P & B Textiles, Hoffman Fabrics and Amy Butler Designs generously provided delicious fabrics to create the quilt projects.

Kay Arnaudo, Laurel Bross, Al Castino, Anna Chan, Christopher Cronin, Eleanor Dugan, Lisa Garrigues, Simcha Greenspan, Ingrid Larson, Mary Lou Keyworth, Chris Pagels, Lydia Pereira, Harry Shonteff and Pam Winter all contributed in smaller, but vital ways to the creation or improvement of this book.

Kelly Biscopink, my wise and gentle editor, has the knack of partnering with an author to make the best possible book. She has made writing it an almost carefree experience!

Thank you all for adding the topstitching that holds this book together.

15 14 13 12 11   5 4 3 2 1

DISTRIBUTED IN CANADA BY FRASER DIRECT
100 Armstrong Avenue
Georgetown, ON, Canada L7G 5S4
Tel: (905) 877-4411

DISTRIBUTED IN THE U.K. AND EUROPE BY F&W MEDIA INTERNATIONAL
Brunel House, Newton Abbot, Devon, TQ12 4PU, England
Tel: (+44) 1626 323200, Fax: (+44) 1626 323319
Email: enquiries@fwmedia.com

DISTRIBUTED IN AUSTRALIA BY CAPRICORN LINK
P.O. Box 704, S. Windsor NSW, 2756 Australia
Tel: (02) 4577-3555

SRN: Y1329
ISBN-13: 978-14402-1552-0

www.fwmedia.com

Edited by Kelly Biscopink

Designed by Julie Barnett

Production coordinated by Greg Nock

Photographed by Christine Polomsky

Styled by Lauren Emmerling

Illustrated by Rhoda Draws

Metric Conversion Chart

to convert	to	multiply by
inches	centimeters	2.54
centimeters	inches	0.4
feet	centimeters	30.5
centimeters	feet	0.03
yards	meters	0.9
meters	yards	1.1

Keep Reading for More Quilt Inspiration!

Great books, fabric, notions and supplies that will have you quilting with ease are just a mouse-click away!

Visit us at store.marthapullen.com

Stash with Splash Quilts

Cindy Casciato

All quilters have a fabric stash at home that they don't know how to use. Quilt along with Cindy Casciato and Nancy Zieman as they share patterns, tips and techniques for making the most of your fabric stash and your favorite splash fabric!

3-Fabric Quilts
Quick Techniques for Simple Projects

Leni Levenson Wiener

In *3-Fabric Quilts*, Leni Levenson Wiener gives you the tools to make twelve fantastic quilts, each requiring only three fabrics. Illustrated instructions, each with yardage requirements for a small and large size, make quilting fun whether you're a beginner or advanced quilter. Choose three fabrics and you're ready to sew!

Become part of the online craft community today!

 Twitter @fwcraft

 Facebook at facebook.com/fwcraft

KRAUSE PUBLICATIONS

3119202031512I